Jesus

and the

Theology of Israel

Zacchaeus Studies: Theology

General Editor: Monika Hellwig

Jesus

and the

Theology of Israel

by

John Pawlikowski

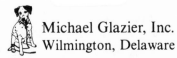

Michael Glazier, Inc.
Wilmington, Delaware

About the Author

John T. Pawlikowski, OSM, is a professor of Social Ethics at the Catholic Theological Union in Chicago. He has written and lectured extensively on Christian-Jewish questions, and he is a co-editor of *Biblical and Theological Reflections on the Challenge of Peace* (Michael Glazier, 1984).

First published in 1989 by Michael Glazier, Inc., 1935 West Fourth Street, Wilmington, Delaware 19805.

Library of Congress Cataloging-in-Publication Data

Pawlikowski, John.
  Jesus and the theology of Israel/John Pawlikowski.
    p. cm.—(Zacchaeus studies. Theology)
    Bibliography: p.
    ISBN 0-89453-683-4
    1. Judaism (Christian theology) 2. Jesus Christ—Views on Judaism.
  I. Title. II. Series.
  BT93.P39 1989
  231.7'6—dc20   88-82453
                                              CIP

Cover Design by Maureen Daney
Typography by Edith Warren
Printed in the United States of America by McNaughton & Gunn, Inc.

Contents

Editor's Note

This series of short texts in doctrinal subjects is designed to offer introductory volumes accessible to any educated reader. Dealing with the central topics of Christian faith, the authors have set out to explain the theological interpretation of these topics in a Catholic context without assuming a professional theological training on the part of the reader.

We who have worked on the series hope that these books will serve well in college theology classes where they can be used either as a series or as individual introductory presentations leading to a deeper exploration of a particular topic. We also hope that these books will be widely used and useful in adult study circles, continuing education and RENEW programs, and will be picked up by casual browsers in bookstores. We want to serve the needs of any who are trying to understand more thoroughly the meaning of the Catholic faith and its relevance to the changing circumstances of our times.

Each author has endeavored to present the biblical foundation, the traditional development, the official church position and the contemporary theological discussion of the doctrine or topic in hand. Controversial questions are discussed within the context of the established teaching and the accepted theological interpretation.

We undertook the series in response to increasing interest among educated Catholics in issues arising in the contemporary church, doctrines that raise new questions in a contemporary setting, and teachings that now call for wider and deeper appreciation. To such people we offer these volumes, hoping that reading them may be a satisfying and heartening experience.

Monika K. Hellwig
Series Editor

1

Twentieth Century Developments in Understanding Jesus' Relationship to Judaism

I. INTRODUCTION

In 1965 Vatican Council II issued its historic declaration on Catholicism's relationship to non-Christian religions entitled *Nostra Aetate* which included a groundbreaking section on the church's continuing links with the Jewish People through Jesus. This statement had a significant impact on both Catholic and Protestant thinking on the Jewish question. *Nostra Aetate* was followed by well over fifty additional statements from individual Christian leaders and regional church bodies in North America, Western Europe and South America. The principal Protestant pronouncements include the 1980 Rhineland Synod statement and the study document entitled "Ecumenical Considerations on Jewish-Christian Dialogue" submitted to its member denominations in 1982 by the World Council of Churches. The Vatican followed *Nostra Aetate* with a set of guidelines for implementing its section on the Jewish People in 1975. These guidelines actually moved us beyond the original conciliar document in some areas. Most recently, in 1985, Rome presented Catholics with *Notes on the Correct Way to Present the Jews and Judaism in Preaching and Catechesis.*[1]

The breakthrough in understanding the Christian-Jewish relationship brought about by Vatican II had a pre-history. Immediately after World War II, and largely as a result of the trauma caused by the annihilation of six million Jews, several prominent European theologians began to explore possibilities for Christian theological affirmation of the Jewish covenant in light of the Christ Event. Names such as Charles Journet, Jean Danielou, Karl Barth, Hans Urs von Balthasar and Augustin Cardinal Bea (an influential figure in the passage of *Nostra Aetate*) stand out. In the United States pioneering work was begun by Msgr. John Oesterreicher with publication of a series of volumes called *The Bridge*.[2] And the concrete experience of Jews and Christians cooperating on many projects in North America, though it did not lead to much systematic theological reflection on the links between Jews and Christians, did stimulate a positive atmosphere for such rethinking. This American experience of constructive religious pluralism proved decisive in the passage of *Nostra Aetate.*

The initial attempts at theological reconstruction of Christian-Jewish relationship began to chip away at two long dominant trends in Christian thought. The first, which predominated in Catholicism (particularly in the liturgy), focused around the prophecy/fulfillment motif. Jesus fulfilled the Messianic prophecies of Judaism and thus inaugurated the messianic era for which Jews had hoped and prayed throughout the centuries. It was their own spiritual blindness that prevented most Jews from recognizing this fulfillment in the Christ Event. As a divine punishment for this blindness Jews were displaced in the

---

[1]A complete collection of these documents can be found in Helga Croner (ed)., *Stepping Stones to Further Jewish-Christian Relations.* London/New York: Stimulus Books, 1977 and *More Stepping Stones to Jewish-Christian Relations.* New York/ Mahwah: Paulist, 1985. For accounts of the development of *Nostra Aetate,* cf. Arthur Gilbert, *The Vatican Council and the Jews.* Cleveland/New York: World, 1968 and John M. Oesterreicher, *The New Encounter Between Christians and Jews.* New York: Philosophical Library, 1986.

[2]Cf. *The Bridge, A Yearbook of Judaeo-ChristianStudies,* Vols. 1-4. New York: Pantheon, 1955 (I), 1956 (II), 1958 (III), and 1961 (IV). Also, *Brothers in Hope; The Bridge,* Vol. V. New York: Herder & Herder, 1970.

covenantal relationship by those baptized into the "New Israel."
The second trend, heavily identified with continental Protestant
theology, saw *freedom* as the principal effect of the Christ Event.
Through his preaching and ministry and in a very special way
through his death/resurrection Jesus freed humankind from the
"burden of Jewish Torah" which was so spiritually inhibiting. The
whole Jewish covenantal experience of the people's union with
God through faithful observance of the Torah precepts integral to
the divine-human bonding forged at Sinai was displaced by the
immediate, individual covenantal union between the individual
believer and God through Christ.

The initial efforts at moving from these "displacement"
theologies of Judaism towards a viewpoint more accepting of an
ongoing post-Easter Jewish covenantal presence continued to
remain uncompromising on the centrality of Christ and the
fulfillment resulting from the Incarnation and the Resurrection.
No real attempt was made to erase the apparent contradiction
between the affirmation of Jewish covenantal continuity and
fulfillment in Christ. Rather these theologians appealed to the
so-called "mystery' theology of the Jewish-Christian relationship
found in chapters 9-11 of Paul's letter to the Romans. Following
Paul's lead, they insisted that the church needs to make these twin
proclamations as part of its fundamental faith statement even
though ultimate reconciliation lies beyond human comprehen-
sion. In other words, it remains a perpetual *mystery* understood
by God alone who remains Sovereign of both Jews and Christians.

Since the time of the Council an increasing number of theologians, and several important church documents, have eased away
from this "mystery" theology. They have offered a model of the
Jewish-Christian relationship in which the notions of the exclusive
centrality of Christ and his complete fulfillment of messianic
prophecies have been modified in varying degrees.

It has become customary to classify the theologians working
within the framework of the Christian-Jewish dialogue as holding
either a *single covenant* or a *double covenant* perspective. The
former conceives of Jews and Christians as basically part of an
ongoing, integrated covenantal tradition appropriated by each in
somewhat different ways. The Christ Event in this view facilitated
the entry of non-Jews into a covenantal relationship Jews never

lost. The double covenant position, on the other hand, emphasizes the distinctiveness of each covenantal tradition but insists that both are ultimately crucial for the complete emergence of the divine reign.

Increasingly the feeling is developing that neither of these two categories adequately express the complexity of the relationship between Christianity and Judaism. But there is nothing approaching consensus on more appropriate classifications. The Vatican, after including its statement on the Jews in the conciliar document on non-Christian religions, located its commission for implementing the document within the Secretariat for Promoting Christian Unity. The World Council of Churches, on the other hand, now deals with Christian-Jewish dialogue within the framework of the broader dialogue between Christians and peoples of other faiths and ideologies.

Behind this Christian institutional uncertainty lies a profound theological question that awaits some resolution. Do we enhance the theological status of Judaism from the Christian perspective by stressing its intimate links with the church or by highlighting its distinctiveness? It is obviously not an either-or question. But it does make a difference which is given the emphasis. Obviously both perspectives wish to retain a close, continuing link between the two covenantal traditions. The dilemma is that the single covenantal tradition runs the risk of a new kind of absorption of Judaism, more benign but still absorption, while the double covenant framework can easily fall prey to the temptation of underplaying Christianity's Jewish roots.

Moving back to *Nostra Aetate* we recognize that this brief statement undercut much of the prevailing theology of Judaism within the church. The document unqualifiedly acknowledges Christianity's profound debt to its Jewish heritage—an indebtedness that continues unabated into our day. Picking up the imagery employed by Paul in Romans 9-11 the Council described the church as grafted onto the tree of salvation whose trunk was Judaism. Such imagery surely implies continued vibrancy for Judaism from a Christian theological perspective. For if the trunk has died, as we sometimes claimed in the past, the branches can hardly stay healthy.

Vatican II did not elaborate a theological perspective on Judaism. But a statement approved at a 1969 plenary session of the episcopal members of the Secretariat for Promoting Christian Unity provides an early indication of the theological directions in which the Council wished Catholicism to move in light of *Nostra Aetate's* proclamation of continued bonding between Israel and the Church. This document understands Judaism to be central to any authentic ecclesiology: "The problem of the relations between Jews and Christians concerns the *church as such,* since it is in "searching into its own mystery' that it comes upon the mystery of Israel."[3] It also affirms the enduring value of the Hebrew Scriptures for Christian faith expression, maintaining that this is in fact the direction set by the New Testament. As a result, Christians must begin to draw upon the resources of the Jewish tradition for interpreting these books.

Another significant point found in this 1969 document concerns the Jewishness of Jesus. His positive appropriation of the Jewish tradition needs to be fully appreciated by Christians today. This reverses a predominant exegetical trend which tended to downplay Jesus' deep involvement with the Jewish community of his time and emphasized the supposed Hellenistic background of New Testament teachings at the expense of the Jewish. This interpretative school also frequently transformed Jesus into a "universal" person, obliterating his links to the Jewish people. In this view Christian faith was seen as primarily rooted in an immediate, personal decision for Jesus with little role for the historically based, communally oriented Jewish covenantal tradition.

Finally, the Catholic bishops' meeting of 1969 brought to our attention another pre-conciliar theological model of the Jewish-Christian relationship that Vatican II had undercut. On the whole, this model was much stronger in Protestant circles than in Catholicism, though the latter was not totally unaffected by its debilitating outlook on Judaism. Succinctly stated, this theological approach contrasted Judaism and Christianity as religions of law and freedom. The prevailing ethos of this description of the

[3]III, a Cf. Croner (ed.), *Stepping Stones,* 3.

Jewish-Christian relationship was the absolute superiority of Christianity which provides the believer with an immediate union with God through the grace given through Christ without the mediation of the law. The new possibility of immedate grace made possible by the Christ Event totally invalidated the Torah approach to religion that stands at the heart of Judaism. Taking their lead from *Nostra Aetate*, the bishops argued that these contrasts no longer represent an appropriate way to describe the link between the two faith communities:

> The Old Testament and Jewish tradition should not be opposed to the New Testament in such a way as to make it appear as a religion of justice alone, a religion of fear and legalism, implying that only Christianity possesses the law of love and freedom.[4]

This cautionary note sounded by the Catholic bishops in 1969 takes on new importance in our time. Presently, we are witnessing some resurgence of this classical Christian attitude towards the Jewish covenant within both liberationist and feminist theologies. Jesus frequently has been presented in their formulations of Christology as the one who freed humankind either from the oppressive structures of the Torah or the patriarchial structures seen as endemic to biblical and Second Temple Judaism.[5]

While both these theological movements highlight forms of structural injustice to which the church and humankind as a whole can no longer remain indifferent, combatting this deep-seated injustice need not involve resurrecting the old law-gospel model repudiated by the spirit of *Nostra Aetate*. A theology of Christian freedom based on the ministry and person of Jesus must not be built on the back of Judaism. For Jesus' spirituality of freedom was very much a child of the central dynamic of the

---

[4]Cf. *Stepping Stones*, 9.

[5]This period begins with the construction of the Second Temple in Jerusalem after Cyrus the Persian granted the Jews a modicum of religious freedom after the Exile. The building of the new Temple is described in the books of Ezra and Nehemiah. It continued until the destruction of the Temple in the Roman War, 64-70 A.D. The latter part of this period has been traditionally called the "inter-testamental" period in Christian writings.

Jewish tradition, especially the Exodus tradition and the developments within Second Temple Judaism. As will be shown later in this volume, Jesus' bonding with Pharisaic Judaism [6] profoundly enriched and shaped his theology and ministry of liberation. Judaism was not an obstacle for Jesus in his quest for human dignity and justice, as some liberation theologians[7] such as Jon Sobrino and Leonardo Boff seem to imply, but a greatly treasured resource.

The decade of the seventies saw the first significant movement away from reliance on the Pauline "mystery" model as the ultimate expression of the continuing link between Christians and Jews. A growing number of Protestant and Catholic theologians began to seek ways of stating this linkage in more positive, explicit ways that involved some modification of classical Christian claims about fulfillment in and through the Christ Event. Their perspectives generally fall into the single or double covenantal frameworks mentioned previously. A few have gone even beyond these, understanding Sinai and the Christ Event as only two of an *undetermined* number of messianic experiences.

II. Single Covenantal Perspectives

Several years ago Monika Hellwig[8] offered some initial ideas regarding a new Christian theology of Judaism from a single

---

[6]The origins of the Pharisees are uncertain. But after the Maccabbean Wars (c. 150 B.C.) they emerge as one of the principal Jewish groups. Traditionally they have been viewed as the arch-enemies of Jesus. But recent scholarship has begun to uncover evidence of a deep, positive relationship between Jesus and at least some parts of the movement. The Pharisees saw themselves as heirs of the prophetic tradition and opposed the Temple system dominated by their chief opponents the Sadduccees (the priestly party).

[7]A theological interpretation of Jesus' message which emerged primarily out of Latin America in the late sixties. It is strongly biblical in orientation and champions social justice and the notion of the "preferential option" for the poor.

[8]Cf. "Christian Theology and the Covenant of Israel," *Journal of Ecumenical Studies* 7(Winter 1970), 37-51 and "From the Jesus of Story of the Christ of Dogma," in Alan T. Davies (ed.), *Antisemitism and the Foundations of Christianity*. New York/ramsey/ Toronto: Paulist, 1979, 118-136.

covenantal perspective, though she has not pursued this question recently. Other single covenantal viewpoints are found in the writings of the Israeli Catholic philosopher Marcel Dubois, O.P., Cardinal Martini of Milan, and, with a somewhat new twist, Michael Remaud. The recent speeches of Pope John Paul II, who in fact has addressed the theological bond between Christianity and Judaism more substantively and creatively than any other pope in history, as well as the *Notes* on Catholic catechesis and Judaism released in 1985, also move in a pronounced single covenantal vein.

In Monika Hellwig's perspective Judaism and Christianity are both envisioned as pointing towards the identical eschatological event[9] which continues to remain very much of a *future* reality. They share a common mission in helping the final eschatological age unfold, though each may carry out this mission in somewhat different ways. But Hellwig clearly understands the implications of the joint vocation she entrusts to Christians and Jews in her theological perspective. All previous claims by the church that Jesus totally fulfilled Jewish messianic beliefs must of necessity be cast aside. Her theological vision is cleary dependent on Christian willingness to acknowledge a most important unfilled dimension to the Christ Event, to admit forthrightly that eschatological tension has not yet been completely resolved. The messianic event for her must be understood as unfinished and mysterious, as lengthy and complex.

Hellwig insists that the covenant forged with Israel at Sinai was not obliterated with the coming of Jesus. It remains fully in force. This affirmation of continuing divine faithfulness to the covenant with the Jewish people forces Hellwig into rethinking the fundamental significance of Jesus as the Christ. Her answer is to see in the Christ Event not primarily the completion of messianic prophecies, but the possibility of all Gentiles encountering the God of Abraham, Sarah, and Isaac. Jesus the Jew opened the gates for Gentiles to enter the covenantal election first granted the

---

[9]This refers to the final period in human history when the ultimate reconciliation between God and all creation is to take place. Traditionally Jews see it as the time when the Messiah will finally arrive and peace and justice will reign. For Christians, it will mark the final culmination begun through Jesus, especially through his Death/Resurrection.

People Israel and to experience the intimacy with God that this election brought them. Hence Christians must look to God's continuing revelation in contemporary Jewish experience to grasp fully God's self-communication today. While some ambiguity remains in Hellwig's thought on this point, she also seems to imply that the revelation given humankind in and through the Christ Event serves as one barometer for Jewish faith expression as well. Her theology of Jewish-Christian linkage thus ultimately involves some rethinking of respective self-definitions by both faith communities.

In more recent writings Hellwig is willing to grant that in the end it does not matter all that much whether we speak of one or two covenants in terms of the Jewish-Christian relationship. The crucial question is whether people in the church describe Christianity as consummating everything valuable in Judaism so that the latter no longer retains any salvific role or whether, instead, Christians understand themselves as simultaneous participants with Jews in an ongoing covenantal relation with God. She still prefers to stay with the vocabulary and imagery of a single covenant because it has a solid biblical basis and contains what she calls "a germ of ecumenism capable of further unfolding." Additionally, she feels that the single covenant notion helps to remind us that there is but one God and one unified, meaningful creation which makes possible communal destiny and fulfillment.

Turning to Marcel Dubois[10] we find a great stress on the Cross as a unifying point for Christians and Jews. The Jesus of Israel finally becomes the crucified Jesus of Israel and it is this Jesus that for Dubois becomes the link between Jews and Christians. Dubois associates Jesus' sufferings on the Cross with those experienced by the Jewish People during the Holocaust, or as Jews now prefer to name this period, *the Shoah* ("annihilation"). For him Jesus completes Israel in its role as the Suffering Servant. And, in turn, Israel symbolizes, even if unconsciously, the mystery of the Passion and the Cross.

Dubois is one of the few Christian theologians to choose to

---

[10]Cf. "Christian Reflections on the Holocaust," SIDIC 7:2 (1974), 10-16 and *Recontres Avec Le Judaisme en Israel.* Jerusalem: Editions de l'Olivier, 1983.

reflect theologically on the Jewish-Christian relationship in the context of a Cross/Shoah nexus. Most scholars have tended to avoid using this framework as the basis of a new constructive theological model of the Christian-Jewish relationship both because of the significant Christian complicity (direct and indirect) in the Holocaust and because, while Jesus' passion and death have always been understood as core elements in a *freely* chosen redemptive mission, the extermination of six million Jews had absolutely no voluntary dimension to it. One other example of such an approach is to be found in Jurgen Moltmann's *The Crucified God*.[11] Here Moltmann tries to build a Christology in which the crucifixion's ultimate meaning becomes apparent in the monumental event that was the Shoah. But Moltmann does not deal directly with the implications of this link for a contemporary theology of the Christian-Jewish relationship.

An interesting new version of the single covenant theory has been proposed by Cardinal Martini of Milan, former head of the Biblicum in Rome.[12] Martini has introduced the idea of "schism" into the discussion of the basic theological relationship between Jews and Christians. He applies this term to the original separation of the church and the synagogue. In so doing he has interjected two important notions into the conversation. For "schism" is a reality that ideally *should not have occurred* (Christianity and Judaism should have remained permanently bonded) and which is seen as a *temporary situation* rather than a permanent rupture. So "schism," which previously has been used exlusively in connection with inter-Christian divisions, implies a certain contemporary mandate to heal this rupture.

Martini also argues that in every previous schism Catholicism has suffered a certain lack of balance in its faith expression. It has been deprived of significant richness. But in no schism, he insists, was this more true than in the original separation with the Jewish People. This break frequently skewed the articulation of Christian faith, in particular faith in Jesus as the Christ, in ways that proved

[11] *The Crucified God.* New York: Harper & Row, 1978.

[12]"The Relation of the Church to the Jewish People," *From the Martin Buber House* 6(1984), 3-10.

detrimental for the church. These are his exact words:

> Every schism and division in the history of Christianity entails the deprivation of the body of the Church from contributions which could be very important for its health and vitality, and produces a certain lack of balance in the living equilibrium of the Christian community. If this is true of every great division in Church history, it was especially true of the first great schism which was perpetrated in the first two centuries of Christianity.[13]

The French Catholic scholar Michael Remaud [14] picks up some of the same themes as the other Catholic theologians, although to date he has offered only a brief sketch of a theological model. He totally discredits any "displacement" theology of the Christian-Jewish relationship or any theology of "substitution" in which the church totally appropriates for itself the covenantal identity of the Jewish People, leaving the latter an empty shell. The unique dimension in Remaud's writings consists in his use of a reinterpreted form of the earlier "mystery" solution to the dilemma of church/synagogue co-existence. Remaud defines "mystery" in a rather novel, creative way in comparison to previous proponents of this perspective. He takes "mystery" to mean essentially "spiritual reality." Both Israel and the Church participate in this same spiritual reality which has several dimensions. Israel's distinctive role is to highlight the messianic hope in this spiritual reality; the church, on the other hand, bears witness to the already existing hope made present through the Christ Event that is central to this one, though complex, spiritual reality.

This contribution by Remaud is intriguing, though in need of much greater elaboration. It represents a possible new way of building a theological model of the Jewish-Christian relationship from Romans 9-11. The proposal, especially in its interpretation of the Pauline sense of "mystery," may in the end fail to bear the

---

[13]Martini, "The Relation," 9.

[14]Cf. *Chrétiens Devant Israël Serviteur de Dieu.* Paris: Cerf, 1983 and *Catholiques et Juifs: Un Nouveau Regard.* Paris: Cerf, 1985.

weight of scholarly scrutiny. But it is to be welcomed as an important contribution to the discussion. It has the decided advantage of providing a continuing, *distinctive* mission for Israel after the Easter event.

Turning to the addresses of Pope John Paul II we quickly recognize that they contain the most extensive, constructive discussion of the theology of the Christian-Jewish relationship yet offered by any pontiff. Throughout his several statements[15] we see a growing emphasis on an intimate, altogether special bond between the Church and the Jewish People. He often speaks of the two communities being "linked at the very level of their identities."[16] And in his remarks to the official Jewish-Catholic delegation assembled in Rome to celebrate the twentieth anniversary of *Nostra Aetate* in October 1985, John Paul stressed even further the depth of this linkage and how it exists with no other world religion:

> It is this "link" . . . that is the real foundation for our relation with the Jewish people. A relation which could well be called a real "parentage" and which we have with that religious community alone, notwithstanding our many connections with other world religions, particularly with Islam. . . . This "link" can be called a "sacred" one, stemming as it does from the mysterious will of God.[17]

The pope re-emphasized this theme of a fundamental bondedness between Judaism and Christianity in his historic visit to Rome's principal synagogue in April 1986. In his remarks that day John Paul said that the church discovers this bond by searching into the mystery of her own existence. He insisted that the Jewish religion must not be seen as "extrinsic" to Christianity but "in a certain way is 'intrinsic' to our own religion." He went on

---

[15]For a summary of important papal statements cf. "Important Declarations of John Paul II," SIDIC XV:2 (1982), 26-28; "Address to Rome's Chief Synagogue," *Origins*, 15:45 (April 1986, 729, 731-733; and "The 20th Anniversary of *Nostra Aetate,"Origins*, 15:25 (December 5, 1985), 409, 411.

[16]Cf. "Important Declarations," 27.

[17]*Origins*, 15:25 (December 5, 1985), 411.

to repeat his *Nostra Aetate* commemoration theme that the church has a relationship with Judaism unlike that with any other religion because of this "intrinsic" link through Christ.[18]

The Vatican *Notes* in addition to picking up the "bonding" language of Pope John Paul II, also speak of a genuine partnership between Christians and Jews in the process of human salvation, as Dr. Eugene Fisher has rightly noted in his commentary on the *Notes* presented at the October 1985 Vatican commemoration.[19] This moves us light years beyond the classical "displacement" model. It clearly makes of the original Christ Event more a future vision of a messianic hope that remains to be completed, partially through human efforts, rather than a totally fulfilled reality. And though they start from different places Jews and Christians meet in this common messianic hope rooted in the original promise to Abraham.

There does seem to be genuine movement in official Catholic circles towards embracing the single covenant model for the Jewish-Christian relationship, although many Vatican theological statements appear to continue with a Christian "absolute superiority" model. In fact, the *Notes* themselves show some definite tension in this regard despite their genuine advances, as a number of Christian and Jewish commentators have pointed out.

Looking now at Protestant Christianity, we see the single covenant model in Bertold Klappert [20] and Peter von der Osten-Sacken.[21] Klappert's goal is to construct a Christological credo devoid of anti-Judaism. Put more positively, such a Christology would involve at its core a continuing link with the Jewish biblical tradition as well as with contemporary Judaism.

Peter von der Osten-Sacken follows much the same line of thought as Klappert. He too stresses that a renewed Christology must affirm the continuity of the Christ Event with both the Hebrew Scriptures and with contemporary Judaism. But he adds

---

[18]Cf. *Common Ground*, 3 (1986), 6.

[19]"The Evolution of a Tradition: From *Nostra Aetate* to the 'Notes,'" *Christian/Jewish Relations*, 18:4 (December 1985), 42-43.

[20]Cf. *Israel Und Die Kirche; Erwägungen Zur Israellehre Karl Barths.* Munich, 1980.

[21]Cf. *Grundzüge Einer Theologie Im Christlich-Jüdischen Gesprach.* Munich, 1982.

an additional image worth noting. For him the best way to express the church's ongoing relationship with the Jewish People theologically is through development of an "Israel-affirming Christology" as a replacement for the old displacement theology.

The most comprehensive theological model for the Jewish-Christian relationship within the Protestant tradition is currently being developed by Paul van Buren. *The Burden of Freedom* was his first, rather preliminary statement in which he primarily emphasized the deficiencies in previous models.[22] This work has been followed by *Discerning the Way*[23], *A Christian Theology of the People Israel*[24] and a recently published statement on Christology entitled *A Theology of the Jewish Christian Reality, Part III: Christ in Context.*[25]

Van Buren argues that Christianity has more or less eradicated all Jewish elements from its faith expression in favor of a pagan—Christian tradition. The Holocaust represents the pinnacle of this impoverished tradition. The church must now rejoin Judaism, no easy task in light of the "cover-up" which van Buren believes took place during the first century of Christian existence. When the Christian leadership realized that the promised signs of the messianic era were nowhere to be seen, the response was not to modify the church's initial theological claims about the Christ Event but rather to push the actual realization of these claims about the advent of the messianic age to a metahistorical, "higher" realm. This metahistorical realm of messianic fulfillment was penetrable through faith. It was not subject to historical verification of any kind. With the completion of this transfer, the path was cleared for the proclamation of the Easter mystery as an unqualified triumph on the part of Christ, a triumph in which the Jewish People held no continuing role.

In his more recent writings van Buren has increasingly insisted that we must recognize that Israel consists of two connected, but

[22]New York: Seabury, 1976.

[23]New York: Seabury, 1980.

[24]New York: Seabury, 1983.

[25]San Francisco: Harper & Row, 1988. Also Cf. "The Context of Jesus Christ: Israel," *Religion & Intellectual Life,* III:4 (Summer 1986), 31-50.

distinct, branches. Both are essential to a full definition of the term "Israel." The Christian church represents the community of Gentile believers drawn by the God of the Jewish People to worship him and to make his love known among the peoples of the world. For Van Buren it is not a question of the church now suddenly abandoning its historic proclamation of Jesus as the Christ and the Son of God. But Jesus was *not* the Christ in one crucial sense. He was not the long-awaited Jewish Messiah. And so post-Easter Judaism remains a religion of legitimate messianic hope rather than of spiritual blindness.

The shared messianic vision of Judaism and Christianity leads van Buren to advocate the notion of the "co-formation" of the two faith communities. By this he means that both of the branches of Israel must grow and develop alongside of each other rather than in isolation. While each will continue to retain a measure of distinctiveness, both will experience a growing mutuality characterized by understanding and love. This growing together in love will increase each partner's freedom to be its distinctive self while maintaining an awareness of the necessity for mutual cooperation.

It has only been after laying some fundamental groundwork in his earlier volumes that Van Buren is beginning to give some in-depth attention to the significance of Christ within his theology of Israel. Van Buren now interprets the new revelation in Jesus as basically the manifestation of the divine will that Gentiles too are welcome to walk in God's way. Through Jesus the Gentiles were summoned for the first time as full participants in the ongoing covenantal plan of salvation. But the Gentiles' appropriation of this plan, van Buren admits, took them well beyond the circles of God's eternal covenant with the Jewish People. In no way, however, did it annul the original covenant. Nor can Christians by-pass the original covenantal people in their quest for bonding with the God of Abraham, Sarah and Isaac who was revealed to them through the ministry and person of the Jew Jesus.

Jesus did not expect a future in the ordinary sense of the word. In that sense his message was ahistorical, much like the rabbis of his period. He anxiously awaited the coming of God's reign which would replace this era. He did reveal a deep, personal intimacy with God, but his relationship with God maintained a clear line of demarcation between himself and the Father. His sense of intimacy with the divine was very Jewish. Van Buren puts it this way:

> We can only speculate about what went on in Jesus' own soul, but we can know how the early witness presents him. It presents him as we could expect Jews to present a Jew wholly devoted to God. It presents him as one whose will was to do God's will. His cause was nothing but the cause of God. In this sense and in no other, he had no will of his own and no cause of his own to defend. In other words, he was strong-willed and stubborn in the cause of God. In short, he was a Jew.[26]

For van Buren any Christological proclamation today, particularly in light of the experience of the Holocaust, musf make it abundantly clear that the divine authorization Jesus enjoyed to speak and act in the name of the Father did not exempt him from the realities of the human condition, and that the powers of death and darkness continued to hold sway after the Easter event. In short, a major modification of many classical Christological claims is demanded by a new understanding of Jesus' relationship to the Jewish community of his day, by the Jewish People's return to historical existence in the modern State of Israel and by the period of *night* we now call "Shoah". If we are to take one traditional Christological doctrine with utmost seriousness, it is the Incarnation. The bishops assembled at the Council of Chalcedon insisted that the Word *became* flesh, not merely that the Word had "put on" flesh. Jesus' participation in the human condition was total and real in every sense of the term.

Where van Buren ultimately winds up on the Christological question is to proclaim Jesus *Israel's gift to the Gentile church.* His primary mission is to reconcile the Gentiles with God. This is still a hard saying for most Christians who remain victims of the church's erroneous first century belief that Jesus was expelled

[26]*Ibid.,* 47.

rather than given by Israel. Van Buren also acknowledges that Jews may have some difficulty with his claim because Judaism has never recognized Jesus as its gift to the church. But this latter situation is largely the result of the sufferings endured for centuries by the Jewish People in the name of Jesus. But as the church begins to move away from the "expulsion" theology of Israel relative to Jesus towards a "gift" theology, Jews will need to rethink their traditional posture towards Jesus as well. For if Israel remains bound to God, and if it is God who gives the church the gift of the Jew Jesus, then Israel remains clearly implicated in this gift.

For the Christian to follow Jesus means to become wholly devoted to the cause of God, especially through love for those very special to God—the poor, the weak, the dispossessed and the oppressed. This is the claim upon Christians inherent in its gift of Jesus from God through Israel. But in accepting Jesus as the gift of God's love, the Gentile church commits itself to a particular love for Israel, God's beloved. If Christians truly wish to follow Jesus, they must consent to care for the least of their brothers and sisters, beginning with the Jewish People. To paraphrase the first letter of John, how can Christians say they really love God whom they have not seen and fail to love Israel whom they have encountered in the flesh and for whom God has so often demonstrated the deepest love?

In giving their special allegiance in faith to Jesus, van Buren tells us, Christians follow, in the words of Paul to the Romans (15:8), a person who "became a servant to the Jewish people." Herein lies the basis of Israel's claim upon Christianity, a claim sealed through Jesus Christ. The church can never escape this profound debt to Israel and profoundly corrupts itself anytime it tries:

> To acknowledge the claim of God's love, with which the church is confronted in the witness to Christ, is therefore always to acknowledge the legitimate claim of Israel. No Jew need repeat that claim today, since it is repeated to the church again and again. whenever it rehearses the things concerning Jesus of Nazareth, by his reality as a Jew. It comes as his call to

follow him in his service to his people.[27]

Moving on now to another major Protestant voice, that of one of the genuine pioneers of the twentieth century Christian-Jewish dialogue, A. Roy Eckardt, we encounter a viewpoint that has tended to shift somewhat over the years. Eckardt has been one of the most prolific writers on the issue of the Christian-Jewish theological relationship beginning with his early work, *Elder and Younger Brothers*.[28] He has also been one of the most radical theologians in terms of a present-day model for the relationship. We will consider his perspective at this point because he certainly began as a proponent of the single covenant approach.

According to Eckardt divine design preordained that a majority of the People Israel would respond negatively to the Christ Event. This was necessary to preserve the continuing integrity of Judaism. Eckardt's longstanding thesis has been that Israel (for him, unlike Van Buren, "Israel" and "the Jewish People" are synonymous) and the church exist in dialectical tension with one another within the framework of a single covenant. Each assumes a different function in the history of salvation and each is prone to a corresponding temptation. Israel's primary role remains to turn inward to the Jewish People while Christianity is outer-directed towards the Gentiles. The corresponding temptations are that the Jews may allow their election to produce self-exaltation, while the church's reliance on grace, on the other hand, can result in a false sense of liberation from all duties prescribed in the Torah. This trend has been especially strong in many Protestant versions of Christology and more recently in many liberationist interpretations of the Christ Event in which Jesus' primary salvific mission consists in giving his followers freedom from the "enslaving" Torah system. Stating these temptations in a more contemporary idiom, Israel, in resisting an exaggerated dichotomy

[27] *Ibid.*, 50.
[28] New York: Schocken, 1973.

between the sacred and the secular,[29] runs the risk of unintentionally oversecularizing the kingdom of God. Christianity meanwhile, in entering the secular world, may overspiritualize the kingdom of God and negate the fundamental link between the sacred and the secular.

For Eckardt Jesus of Nazareth both separates and unites Jews and Christians. Israel's election finds a certain continuity and fufillment in the Incarnation. Eckardt does acknowledge a certain uniqueness about the revelation in Jesus Christ. But in principle, he insists, this revelation is no more significant in the final analysis than the revelation accorded to the Jewish People in the Hebrew Scriptures. There is only one sense in which Christians can speak about fulfillment through the Christ Event: Jesus' ministry forever shattered the wall separating Jews and Gentiles. The enduring covenant with Israel was unlocked for entry by the Gentiles in a way that Judaism never imagined possible.

As we turn to Eckardt's later writings we discover some decided turns that first take him way from a single covenant perspective and then seem to return him to it though in a significantly reformulated way. He first admits that his endorsement of a single covenant viewpoint in the past was due in great measure to his desire to undercut traditional Christian supersessionist theologies of Judaism. As a result, should the church finally arrive at the point where it finds itself fully liberated from the temptation to define itself as Israel's replacement, then it might be possible for the two communities to go their separate ways while maintaining a relationship of mutual love and respect. Eckardt at this point seems willing to make room for the emergence of a model for the Jewish-Christian relationship that would make the two faith communities clearly distinctive entities. This would seem to set him against the dominant stream of "intimate identity" found in current official Catholic teaching and in some major Protestant documents.

---

[29]The term "secular" generally refers to that realm of human activity not directly related to divine activity. It tends to connote areas of human life where a transcendent dimension is not visible. For some, secularity is merely a neutral term with no antireligious overtones. But others often see it as part of a mind-set that refuses to acknowledge a transcendent dimension to all human activities ultimately rooted in God's all-embracing presence.

Most recently Eckardt, in light of his intensified reflection on the Holocaust, has suggested that both traditional notions of covenant and the doctrine of the Resurrection have been rendered obsolete by this watershed theological event. After the Shoah only one type of covenant can continue to be applied to the People Israel in his judgment. That covenant Eckardt describes as "the covenant of divine agony." It is covenantal relationship marked by radical secularity. It is not clear in Eckardt's writings whether he believes the church also can participate in this covenant of secularity, though he seems to suggest that unqualified secularity is indeed the fundamental condition in which Christians also find themselves after the Holocaust.

About the doctrine of Christ's Resurrection in light of the Holocaust Eckardt exhibits little uncertainty. The Shoah clearly showed the error of any completed notion of Resurrection. Resurrection with regard to Jesus remains a totally future category. This future resurrection of Jesus will carry special meaning for Christians because it is his history through which the Gentiles were able to enter the ongoing covenant with Israel. In parallel fashion the future resurrection of Abraham and Moses will take on a distinctive meaning for the eschatological community of Jews.

These latest reflections on the Jewish-Christian relationship appear to return Eckardt to the single covenant camp albeit in a radically new way. Jews and Christians now stand united in their experience of radical secularity. This move, however, would also open up possibilities for links between Eckardt's viewpoint and the multiple covenant position that we shall discuss shortly. For the new secular bondedness that Christians and Jews share seems in principle open to peoples from other classical faith perspectives.

A final version of the single covenant perspective deserving of some discussion is that presented by J. Coos Schoneveld. He joins van Buren and Eckardt in arguing that the basic meaning of the Christ Event fundamentally consists in its unveiling for the Gentiles the plan of human salvation revealed to the Jewish People through Abraham and Moses. But while van Buren and Eckardt remain somewhat ambiguous on the question of entirely new revelation in and through Christ, Schoneveld makes his position quite clear. Nothing essentially different is added by the New Testament to what is already found in the Torah. Emphases and expression may somewhat vary but the substance of belief is the same. Christians share in the promises originally made to Israel and exhibit their faithfulness to these promises in ways other than those developed by the Jewish community. In some respects the Christian response allows for greater flexibility. But in no way is it superior or based on substantially new insights into the divine plan of salvation.

For Schoneveld it is illegitimate for Christians to refer to Jesus as the Messiah. His coming did not bring about the promised realities of the messianic kingdom. Thus it is unfair for Christians to reformulate these realities to try to prove that it did. Through Jesus the Gentiles have been invited to share in the divine promises and the range of the teaching of Torah has vastly expanded. Schoneveld calls Jesus "Torah in the flesh." He embodied Torah and made its ultimate meaning transparent to the Gentiles: to bring about a kind of human existence in which the image of God becomes clearly visible. Schoneveld puts it in these words:

> When the Jew says 'Torah,' the Christian says 'Christ,' and basically they say the same thing, although they express it very differently. Both Jews and Christians are called to walk in the path of the Torah, the teaching of the God of Israel which is the Way, the Truth and the Life. The Jews walk this path incorporated in the people of Israel and participating in the Covenant of Sinai by observing the *Mitzvot* .... The Christians walk this path incorporated in the body of Christ, the faithful Jew who was himself the embodiment of Torah and participating in his life, cross and resurrection through the sacraments and the life of faith.[30]

---

[30]"Is the Messiah the Crucial Issue Between Jews and Christians?" Jerusalem Seminar Paper. Bergen, Netherlands: Instituut voor Internationale Excursies, 10-11; "Postscript and Preface," *Immanuel,* 12 (Spring 1981), 152-159; "Israel and the Church in Face of God: A Protestant Point of View," *Immanuel* 3 (Winter 1973/74), 80-83; and "The Jewish 'No' to Jesus and the Christian 'Yes' to Jews," *Quarterly Review,* 4:4 (Winter 1984), 52-63.

Israel and the Church stand together in awaiting the fulfillment of the Torah, that day when the image of God will be seen in all of humanity. The same God judges the faithfulness of both. The Jews express their faithfulness by rejecting the church which tried to strip them of their Torah. Christians, on the other hand, demonstrate their faithfulness through a "yes" to Jesus who embodied the Torah, and therefore a "yes" to the Jewish People with whom he was inseparately linked.

Before ending our consideration of single covenantal perspectives a word should be said about two documents from Protestant church bodies. The 1982 World Council of Churches' document had an interesting evolution. In its preliminary drafts it had a decidedly single covenantal direction. In its final published version, however, it adopts a more neutral stance, merely referring to the theological discussion about various models without endorsing any one of the models. In this sense it differs significantly from the position taken in the 1985 Vatican *Notes* where a definite preference is stated for a unitary covenantal model.

There is no doubt that the strongest institutional theological statement to date on the Jewish-Christian bond appears in the document prepared by the Synod of the Protestant Church of the Rhineland (Federal Republic of Germany) in 1980. It has generated considerable discussion, some of it highly critical.

Two confessional statements are central to this document:

> (1) We confess Jesus Christ the Jew, who as Messiah of the Jews is the Savior of the world and binds the peoples of the world to the people of God.
>
> (2) We believe in the permanent election of the Jewish People as the people of God and realize that through Jesus Christ the church is taken into the covenant of God with His people.[31]

Generally speaking the Rhineland Synod's viewpoint has been welcomed rather warmly by most theologians associated with the process of constructively rethinking the Jewish-Christian rela-

[31]Cf. Helga Croner (ed.), *More Stepping Stones,* 207-209.

tionship. But a major criticism has been voiced by at least one such scholar, namely, Paul van Buren. He has little hesitation giving strong endorsement to the second affirmation quoted above. But he is unwilling to endorse the first one. Van Buren insists that the function of binding the Gentiles to the Jewish People has never been conceived of as a characteristic of the Messiah in Judaism.

Van Buren is correct in this critique. But the first assertion must be rejected on even more fundamental grounds. Jesus is not the expected Jewish Messiah and thus the Rhineland document ultimately builds its model of the Jewish-Christian relationship on some very shaky ground. Because of this serious fundamental weakness I do not accord the document the same groundbreaking status for the question of Jesus and the theology of Israel as some others in the Christian-Jewish dialogue.

From the above analysis it is evident that the single covenant perspective shows many internal differences. It has far from a univocal outlook on Jesus' relationship to Judaism. But all its adherents do share common understandings. These include the following: a firm belief that Gentiles can ultimately be saved only through linkage with the Jewish covenant, something made possible in and through the Christ Event; a sense that the "uniqueness" of Christianity consists far more in modes of expression than in content; and the conviction that Jews and Christians share equally and integrally in the ongoing process of humankind's salvation.

III. Double Covenant Perspectives

Turning our focus now to the double covenant model we find various versions of it as well within Catholic and Protestant theological circles. There is no more consistency in this school than among the single covenant theologians. This position seems to be favored by a majority of Catholic scholars in the dialogue, including Gregory Baum, Clemens Thoma and Franz Mussner. Its prominent supporters in the Protestant community include such names as James Parkes and J. Coert Rylaarsdam.

One of this century's early pioneers in the effort of rethinking Christianity's theological stance toward the Jewish People in light of the Christian event was the Anglican James Parkes. Over the years Parkes developed his outline of the double covenant theory on the basis of what he regarded as the two different but complementary revelations given humankind through Sinai and Calvary respectively.[32]

The Sinai experience Parkes understood to be basically communal in nature, while Calvary focused far more directly on the individual person's link with God. What occurred at Sinai was the full development of a long, gradual growth in humanity's perception of community. Calvary, on the other hand, represents the completion of a process that goes back to exilic Judaism,[33] where there began a growing concern with the destiny of the individual Israelite over and above the ongoing concern with the fate of the People Israel as a whole.

Parkes remained convinced that the revelation unveiled through Calvary in no way replaced Sinai, a claim frequently made for the Christ Event throughout church history. But neither could Sinai merely absorb this new revelation without some fundamental alterations. In the life and teaching of Jesus the two revelations co-exist in creative tension. Jesus' abiding concern with the individual as person does nothing to vitiate the importance of the gradual completion in history of the initial revelation associated with Sinai. Judaism and Christianity are thus inextricably bound to each other as equals. Here Parkes is certainly close to some of the recent language of Pope John Paul II and the Vatican *Notes*. The tension that remains between the church and the Jewish People is rooted in something other than a metaphysic forced upon history from without. Rather it is symbolic of the perennial and inevitable experience of tension in ordinary human

---

[32]Cf. *Judaism and Christianity.* Chicago: University of Chicago Press, 1948 and *The Foundations of Judaism and Christianity.* London: Vallentine-Mitchell, 1960. Also cf. my essay, "The Church and Judaism: The Thought of James Parkes," *Journal of Ecumenical Studies* 6(Fall 1969), 573-597.

[33]The period in Jewish history beginning in the eighth century B.C. and continuing roughly until five hundred B.C. when Jews were granted permission to re-establish themselves as a religious community and rebuild the Jerusalem Temple.

life between the human person as social being and individual creature, as an ultimate value in himself, as formed uniquely in the image of God. Parkes maintained that this tension extends to the whole of life and would continue until the final age. Hence the enduring bond between Jews and Christians would also include a permanent gulf as well. The Christ Event was the root cause of both.

One area in which Parkes' model has been frequently faulted is the scriptural. It does not seem to many commentators clearly enough rooted in scriptural data. This certainly is not the case, however, with the second of our double covenant perspectives, that of J. Coert Rylaarsdam. His approach is developed almost entirely out of the scriptural tradition.[34] He argues that any adequate theological viewpoint regarding the Jewish-Christian relationship must begin by clearly recognizing the presence of two distinctive covenants *within* the Hebrew Scriptures.

The first of these covenants, the one with Israel, focused on God's union with the covenanted community in history. At its core stood a mutual pact of faithfulness and responsibility between God and the Jewish People. This covenant was future-oriented. Divine intervention in history in behalf of the chosen people was an ongoing, open-ended process. Since its basic elan did not mesh well with initial proclamations of finality in the Christ Event within the apostolic church, it tended to be downplayed by the New Testament writers.

The second covenant revolved around the figure of David. It bore a far more eschatological cast. In this covenantal strain religious meaning was rooted in the holiness tradition associated with Mount Zion and the divine presence revealed through the Davidic dynasty. It looked to and celebrated a supra-temporal order of meaning. God was depicted as king of creation and of the nation. The earlier biblical stress on Torah[35] and history is largely

---

[34]"Jewish-Christian Relationship: The Two Covenants and the Dilemmas of Christology," *Journal of Ecumenical Studies,* 9(Spring 1972), 239-260.

[35]"Torah": This is one of the central notions in Judaism. It is nearly impossible to translate adequately into English. We usually render it as "law," but this is only a part of its meaning. It includes history, religious concepts, and ethical teachings as well. For the Jew it also indicates a sense of living faith and deep spirituality.

abandoned. The tension between these two covenantal traditions in the late biblical Judaism led, Rylaarsdam believes, to the growth of several sectarian religious groups. One of these was the eschatologically oriented Christian church which arose out of the preaching of Jesus. This new faith community quickly found itself beset with some of the same tensions as Judaism. But in early Christianity the Davidic covenantal tradition rapidly assumed prominence.

Rylaarsdam thus posits the existence of twin biblical covenants. But they are not two chronologically successive covenants in the way Christians have traditionally explained them. Rather these two covenantal traditions permeate both the Hebrew Scriptures and the New Testament. Recognition of these simultaneous rather than consecutive covenants forces upon the church a radical reshaping of its understanding of the significance of the Christ Event and its consequent model of the Jewish-Christian relationship. For if both Judaism and Christianity continue to revolve around the same two covenants that are intimately related to each other, albeit in a paradoxical fashion, then the church-synagogue relationship, whatever its specific tensions at any given moment, must be understood as one of mutual interdependence.

A final Protestant viewpoint comes from the process theologian Clark Williamson.[36] His position is difficult to categorize within the single/double covenant frameworks, though he appears closer to the double covenant position since he does not use the bonding language between Jews and Christians common to single covenant theologians to any great extent. On the other hand, neither does he try to develop unique features in the original revelation of the Christ Event, a paramount feature of most double covenant viewpoints. In fact, he explicitly disagrees with these attempts, preferring to concentrate on the "present Christ" rather than the historical Christ. He is convinced that all efforts at developing a theology of Christian uniqueness in and through the Christ Event inevitably wind up creating a funda-

---

[36]Cf. "Old Wine in New Skins? A Critique of Modern Christology." Paper presented to the The Schristian Study Group of Judaism and the Jewish People, New York, October 4, 1985 and *Has God rejected his people?* Nashville: Abingdon, 1982.

mentally anti-Judaic Christology.

For Williamson the church's preaching about Jesus the Jew enables Christians to know the God of love and justice whom was first revealed to Israel and whom Israel continues to know. So for Williamson Christ represents no essentially new revelation about God that Jews did not already possess. So in a sense Christianity is basically Judaism for the Gentiles, as it is for many of the single covenant theologians. But he leaves the impression that despite their unity in the God first revealed to Israel Jews and Christians remain two rather distinctive religious communities. One senses no urgency in his theology for a model of the Jewish-Christian relationship expressed in terms of bonding and intimacy. Rather the two communities simply exist side-by-side while recognizing their ultimate unity in God.

The current theological scene in Catholicism shows several continuing efforts to rethink the church's classic displacement theology as the inevitable by-product of Christological revelation. Of these Gregory Baum's[37] is the least developed. Thus far he has merely laid out some principles he considers essential for such a new Christian theology vis-a-vis Judaism. Two cardinal ones are: (1) Judaism is not destined to disappear after the coming of Christ, but continues to play a pivotal role in the completion of the divine salvific plan. God's saving presence remains alive within the Jewish People after the Resurrection; and (2) central to any reformulated Christology that aims at affirming the ongoing theological significance of Judaism must be the abandonment of any claim that Jesus is the one mediator without whom salvation is impossible to attain.

Baum would seem to retain a central significance for the Christ Event in his theology that definitely goes beyond mere Gentile appropriation of the ongoing covenant with Jews as proposed by van Buren or understanding of Israel's God as suggested by

[37]"The Jews, Faith and Ideology," *The Ecumenist* 10(1971/72), 71-76; "The Doctrinal Basis for Jewish-Christian Dialogue," *The Month,* 224 (1967, 232-245; "Introduction" to Rosemary Ruether's *Faith and Fratricide.* , New York: Seabury, 1974; "Rethinking the Church's Mission after Auschwitz," in Eva Fleischner (ed), *Auschwitz: Beginning of a New Era?* New York: Katv, The Cathedral of St. John the Divine, Anti-Defamation League, 1977, 113-128; and "Catholic Dogma After Auschwitz," in Alan T. Davies (ed.), *Antisemitism,* 137-150.

Williamson. Baum claims a *universal* significance for the Christ Event though he offers something other than the classical interpretation of this universalism. What occurred in the Christ Event was the realization that God's full victory is assured, even though not totally realized at present. Hence all messianic claims must be spoken of in terms of the future. Jesus will become the Christ in the full sense only at the onset of the eschatological era.

Baum certainly creates theological space for Judaism and other world religions as well. But there is a decided weakness in his approach as articulated thus far, for he assigns no distinctive role to Judaism and the other religions. This can easily expose him to the charge that rather than creating a new theological model for the Jewish-Christian relationship he has merely pushed the old displacement model to the onset of the eschatological era.

A somewhat more biblically-based version of double covenant which likewise highlights unique features in the Christ Event appears in the works of Clemens Thoma.[38] Thoma emphatically rejects any attempt to describe the basic theological tension between the Church and Israel as rooted in the acceptance/ rejection of Jesus. There was no consistent, univocal notion of the messiah in Jewish thought at the time of Jesus. Many diverse understandings were floating about in a period of great creative renewal within Judaism. Some Jews had even reached the conclusion that the notion of messiah should be permanently discarded. Hence there exists no one Jewish expectation to which Jesus can be compared and no grounds for alleging Jewish rejection of Jesus' fulfillment of this expectation.

For Thoma the uniqueness of Jesus is ultimately located in the unqualified fashion in which he tied the kingdom of God to his own activities and person. In so doing he was following a trend already present in apocalyptic interpretations of Judaism. But his sense of intimacy with the Father went beyond what any branch of Judaism was prepared to acknowledge.

---

[38]*A Christian Theology of Judaism,* trans. by Helga Croner. New York/Ramsey: Paulist, 1980.

A third important Catholic voice within the double covenant school is the German theologian Franz Mussner.[39] His perspective bears many similarities to Thoma's. He shares the same conviction about Jesus' deep, positive links to the Jewish tradition. He likewise rejects any interpretation of the Christ Event over against Judaism in terms of Jesus' fulfillment of biblical messianic prophecies. Rather the uniqueness of the Christ Event arises from the complete identity of the work of Jesus, as well as his words and actions, with the work of God. As a result of the revelatory vision in Christ, the New Testament is able to speak about God with an anthropomorphic boldness not found to the same degree in the Hebrew Scriptures.

In answer to the question of what the disciples finally experienced through their close association with Jesus, Mussner speaks of "a unity of action extending to the point of congruence of Jesus with God, an unheard-of existential imitation of God by Jesus."[40] But this imitation, Mussner insists, is quite in keeping with Jewish thinking, a contention that many Jewish scholars would no doubt challenge. The uniqueness of Jesus is to be found in the *depth* of his imitation of God. So the most distinctive feature of Christianity for Mussner when contrasted with Judaism is the notion of Incarnation rather than fulfillment of the messianic prophecies. And even this Christian particularity is an outgrowth of a sensibility profoundly Jewish at its core.

Having laid out the basic principles of his approach to a theological expression of the Jewish-Christian relationship, Mussner amplifies his model with a discussion of what he calls "prophet Christology" and "Son Christology." The "prophet Christology" is chronologically the older of the two Christologies. It views Jesus as belonging to the line of prophets who manifested the "pathos" of God and joined their words and actions to the divine plan for human salvation. Christianity never completely

---

[39] *Tractate on the Jews: The Significance of Judaism for Christian Faith,* trans. with an introduction by Leonard Swidler. Philadelphia: Fortress Press, 1984 and "From Jesus the 'Prophet' to Jesus 'the Son,'" in Abdoldjavad Falaturi, Jacob J. Petuchowski and Walter Strolz (eds.), *Three Ways to the One God. The Faith Experience in Judaism, Christianity and Islam.* New York: Crossroad, 1987, 76-85.

[40] Mussner, *Tractate,* 226.

abandoned this "prophet Christology," not even in the gospel of John where the "Son Christology" most clearly predominates. The two Christologies do not stand in fundamental opposition. But the "Son Christology" adds a dimensions of superiority to Jesus as prophet that makes the differentiation between Christian and Jewish belief more pronounced.

But even this "Son Christology" in Mussner's analysis has some roots in the Jewish tradition. The claims in the past for an essentially non-Jewish basis for this "high" Christology are unfounded. This "Son Christology" owes much of its language and imagery to the Wisdom literature. Mussner has no illusions that calling attention to the connection between "Son Christology" and the Jewish tradition will remove all opposition to it on the part of Jews. But such an understanding might provide an opening for discussing the issue within the framework of the Christian-Jewish dialogue.

A final Catholic theologian whose work must be noted is Johannes-Baptist Metz.[41] He has not written extensively on the subject. But when he has, it has been with considerable passion and with the unwavering conviction that the experience of the Shoah makes any continued proclamation of a Christology that entirely absorbs or obliterates the Jewish People totally immoral.

After the Shoah Metz is convinced that Christian theology must be guided by the insight that "Christians can form and sufficiently understand their identity only in the face of the Jews."[42] This involves as well a definite reintegration of Jewish history and Jewish beliefs into Christian theological consciousness and statement. Jewish history is not merely Christian pre-history, but an integral, continuing part of ecclesial history. And Jewish belief, in terms of both mode and content, must assume a central place in Christian faith expression. For Metz the critical theological question in light of the Shoah experience is the presence/ absence of God. Obviously any Christological statement is highly

---

[41] *The Emergent Church.* New York: Crossroad, 1981 and "Facing the Jews: Christian Theology after Auschwitz," in Elisabeth Schussler-Fiorenza and David Tracy (eds.), *The Holocaust as Interruption. Concilium* 175, 5 (1984), Edinburgh: T & T. Clark, 1984, 26-33.

[42] "Facing the Jews," 26.

dependent on how we finally resolve the God question. But such resolution is impossible for the Christian without some direct link with the contemporary reflections upon God by the Jews today, a people for whom the Shoah represented the threshold of communal extinction.

With respect specifically to Christology Metz's thought is far less developed than the other theologians we have examined in this survey. He would appear to fall closer to the double covenant viewpoint since he seems to posit some new revelation in Christ that goes beyond the mere entry of the Gentiles into the ongoing covenant established at Sinai. He briefly develops the idea of two modes of believing in the New Testament. One he terms the Pauline mode which has tended to predominate in Christianity for most of its history. The other he calls the synoptic mode. This latter form of belief he basically identifies with the tradition of the Hebrew Scriptures. But he strongly emphasizes that it is a crucial element in New Testament faith as well. The problem is that the dominant trends in Christian theology have pretty much pushed it to the fringes of Christian consciousness. This must now change in Metz's judgment. Thus the first step in solving the problem of Christology and Judaism, as Metz sees it, is for the church to recapture this Hebraic mode of belief. This will in turn profoundly affect the shape of Christological expression, resulting in the elimination of the "victorious" Christology that had all the answers and no further room or need for the Jewish People. It will lead to a future-oriented, open-ended approach to Christology in which the central theme will be discipleship. It will be a Christology expressed in the Hebraic mode of belief, in narration and discipleship stories. It will likewise be a Christology which sees an essential eschatological role for the Jewish People. Metz does not interpret this eschatological role for the Jews in the same way as many fundamentalist Christians who emphasize Jewish conversion as integral to the final age. Rather, following the lead of the great Protestant theologian Karl Barth, Metz argues that the primal "ecumenical" unity we seek as Christians is with the Jews. Only through such a unity, such a partnership, which can then open up into an expanding partnership with other world religions, can the eschatological reign of God fully emerge.

From this cursory examination of double covenant theologies

it should again be evident that there exist numerous variations with no one interpretation clearly dominant. There appears, however, to be some coalescence around the notion that the uniqueness of the revelation in the Christ Event fundamentally consists in a new sense of intimacy between God and humanity. This viewpoint is found, albeit in differing ways, in Parkes, Thoma, Mussner and to an extent in Rylaarsdam. In maintaining this sense of uniqueness for Christianity the double covenant theologians are seemingly more faithful to the New Testament data which appears to indicate an awareness of the early church leadership, even those espousing the pro-Jewish views of the Jerusalem community, that humanity had glimpsed a deepened vision of the God-humankind relationship. The basic difficulty facing these theologians is how, after proclaiming this uniqueness, the bond with Judaism can be maintained in a way that provides for a permanent, special role for Judaism in the salvific process. Otherwise the double covenant viewpoint risks turning Jesus into a barrier rather than a bond between Jews and Christians. Otherwise the double covenant viewpoint might simply be a case of postponing Christian notions of Jewish fulfillment/displacement to the end-time, rather than a genuine reinterpretation of the theology of the Jewish-Christian relationship. Parkes and Rylaarsdam have made some attempt to address this. But this is something that Baum, Thoma and Mussner still need to address more fully.

IV. Multi-Covenantal Viewpoints

The third, most recent, position relative to a proper theological model for framing the Jewish-Christian relationship within a Christological context argues that Sinai and the Christ Event represent two among an undetermined number of messianic experiences within humanity. Rosemary Ruether and Paul Knitter have articulated this perspective in somewhat different tones.

Ruether[43] strongly feels that no new positive theology of Judaism is possible in Christianity without a major overhaul of traditional Christology. She focuses in particular on the anti-Jewish Christologies created by the Church Fathers. These must be eradicated if we are to have genuine theological development in the Jewish-Christian relationship. Likewise she believes the church must drop its claims about Christ inaugurating the mesianic age in any form. Jesus for her is not the Jewish messiah, but a Jew who hoped for the kingdom of God and who died with that hope still unfulfilled. Jesus' ministry did provide a future vision of messianic glory. The man Jesus stands as a model of the hope that this eschatological ideal is in fact capable of achievement. Through Jesus we Christians have a proleptic or anticipatory glimpse of the messianic era that will come about only at the end-time. Jesus as the Christ represents the unification of the human community with its ultimate destiny which is yet to come and in whose life and death the world witnessed a struggle for the realization of that unity.

But the Christ Event constitutes an authentic eschatological paradigm only for the people who have consciously accepted it as such. Others who have turned to alternate paradigms which have emerged compellingly from central experiences in their own respective histories should not be looked upon by Christians as unredeemed. The Exodus Event, for example, does the same for Jewish identity that the Christ Event does for Christianity. It is the foundation of hope and a statement about the ultimate conquerability of evil. The Christ Event in no way invalidates the value of the Exodus experience as a paradigm, nor vice versa. Each speaks to a different group of people.

A recent contribution to the rethinking of Christianity's relationship to Judaism and other world religions that falls into the radical category along with Ruether's writings is Paul Knitter's *No Other Name?* [44] Knitter proposes a theocentric Christological model which revolves around a notion of "relational uniqueness"

---

[43] *Faith and Fratricide* (cf. n. #30) "An Invitation to the Jewish-Christian Dialogue: In What Sense Can We Say That Jesus was 'The Christ'?", *The Ecumenist* 10(January/February 1972), 14-19.

[44] *No Other Name?* Maryknoll, NY: Orbis, 1985.

for Jesus. This uniqueness is primarily characterized by its
potential inclusiveness with respect to other religious figures even
though the Christ Event is not automatically normative for all
peoples:

> Jesus is unique, but with a uniqueness defined by its ability to
> relate to—that is, to include and be included by—other unique
> religious figures. Such an understanding of Jesus views him
> not as exclusive or even as normative but as theocentric, as a
> universally relevant manifestation (sacrament, incarnation) of
> divine revelation and salvation.[45]

Knitter goes on to insist, however, that such uniqueness claims
for Jesus cannot be presumed, but must be tested through
concrete dialogoue with other world religions.

Knitter thus stands somewhere on a bridge between Ruether
and the double covenant theologians. He is somewhat responsive
to Ruether's attempt to relativize the authentic messianic hope
associated with the Christ Event, but in the end he leaves open the
possibility for a universality in this event that she seems to exclude
from the outset. They do agree on the point that Christianity can
never assume this universal significance of the Christ Event when
relating to Judaism or any other world religion. Such universality
depends on its affirmation by another religious tradition.

As a Christian theologian Knitter seems prepared in principle
to place the fundamental orienting experiences of Judaism and
other world religions more or less on a par with the Christ Event.
Since his basic goal is to develop principles for a theology of
religious pluralism, he does not really consider the question of
what unique features Judaism or any other world religion might
bring to Christianity's self-awareness.

What can we say in summary of these two attempts to recast
the discussion of Christology and Judaism in a profound way?
There is little doubt that Ruether's writings have been responsible
for raising the Christogical question to a new centrality in the
dialogue. She surely has made a most important contribution in

[45]*Ibid.*, 171-172.

her bold challenge to simplistic classical Christian claims that Jesus fulfilled the major Jewish messianic hopes. And she has brought out very well the shadow side of christology, the destructive features of the church's attempt to argue that this fulfillment took place in a "higher" realm, when it became obvious to everyone that any talk of fulfillment within history would not stand the test of evidence. Her insistence that Christian faith needs to be replanted firmly within history can be enthusiastically endorsed.

On balance, however, she must be judged to have relativized the Christ Event far too much. And she has in no way probed the revelations of the Exodus and the Christ Event to see whether they are in any way complementary to each other. To some extent she has presented us with false options relative to Christology and Judaism. We do not have to continue allegiance to the traditional fulfillment/superiority model for the Christ Event relative to Judaism in order to retain a claim that there is a measure of uniqueness for the Christ Event and centrality that does not by definition rule out other central events. In other words there are possible positions between her radical surgery and the mere affirmation of the traditional claims *in toto*.

Knitter's approach, though less developed with regard to the specifics of a possible Christian-Jewish theological model, has greater possibilities for application in a constructive fashion. But it needs major development. For one, Knitter has not really considered the question of the special link between Judaism and Christianity which seems not to exist between Christianity and any other world religion with the possible exception of Islam. Secondly, Knitter needs to probe much further the potential contribution of Judaism (and other world religions for that matter) to Christian faith awareness in much more specific terms than he has done to date.

V. Additional Perspectives

To round off this discussion of recent developments in Christology and Judaism, as a lead-in to the next chapter with its presentation of a new constructive model of the Christology-

Judaism relationship, it would prove useful to focus on three outlooks which are a required prelude for further advancement in this area. The first concerns the treatment of New Testament data relative to the Christ Event. With Franz Mussner we need to acknowledge a gradual evolution in Christological awareness in the New Testament, away from what I would term "Messianic fulfillment" Christology and he calls "prophet" Christology, found chiefly in the synoptic gospels, towards "consciousness" Christology or "Son" Christology in Mussner's idiom, which dominates the gospel of John and the later Pauline writings.[46] Raymond Brown also speaks in similar terms about early Christological development, though he explicitly associates it with liturgical experiences.[47] What is especially critical here is the methodology, the principle of interpretation that we employ relative to these two basic Christological strains in the New Testament. Unless we are prepared to begin with the methodological assumption that not everything in the New Testament is of equal value for contemporary faith expression, we will not get very far in Christological revision relative to Judaism. Accepting this assumption at the outset will enable us to use the later "Son" or "consciousness" Christology as our starting point for a constructive theology of Judaism, rather than the earlier New Testament proclamations about the meaning of the Christ Event whose *fulfillment* stress seems to eradicate an ongoing salvific role for the Jewish People.

At the heart of the second requisite outlook is the affirmation of the fundamentally developmental, rather than static, nature of revelation. We are continually being offered new revelatory insights as the church advances the building of the kingdom through its participation in the flow of history. This outlook is equally crucial, for it allows us once again to base our contemporary theology of the Christ Event on "Son" Christology rather than "fulfillment" Christology. We feel justified in so doing.

[46]"In speaking of this Christological development, we must not lose sight of actual NT composition. The Pauline letters by and large are earlier than the gospels in their final form. The gospels, especially John, seem to include disparate strands that were finally put together well after Paul's death.

[47]Cf. Raymond E. Brown, "Does the New Testament Call Jesus God?" *Theological Studies,* 26:4 (December 1965), 538-551.

And this is not due merely because historically "Son" Christology seems far more the result of mature apostolic reflection than initial faith enthusiasm but in the main because subsequent revelation through historical experience has convinced the Christian community of the weakness of any fulfillment claims relative to the Christ Event in view of the continued presence of evil and sufferings, a point made eloquently by Rosemary Ruether, and the tenacious vitality of the Jewish People despite the trauma of events such as the Nazi Holocaust.

The third outlook involves the willingness to move beyond an attitude of toleration with respect not only to Judaism but to all world religions as well. It means the firm commitment to a positive affirmation of religious pluralism. Such a constructive theological approach to religious diversity may not necessarily demand the wholesale abandonment of eschatological truth claims, as Israeli scholar David Hartman has insisted is the case. But surely at the minimum it will require the discarding of the kind of "spiritual monism" which Hartman has rightly seen as a deep cancer in any faith tradition:

> We have to recognize that ultimately spiritual monism is a disease. It leads to the type of spiritual arrogance that has brought bloodshed to history. Therefore we have to rethink our eschatology, and rethink the notion of multiple spiritual communities and their relationship to a monotheistic faith.[48]

We may continue to regard our respective claims to truth as central for the redemption of humanity. But no longer can we look upon them as exclusively so. A measured recognition that our truth claims remain incomplete must begin to penetrate human self-awareness, an incompleteness that can be overcome only by deep and respectful encounter with other religious traditions. Other religious traditions exist for our own spiritual enrichment as well as that of their own adherents, for our salvation as well as their own. This stands as a key principle for any meaningful and enduring theology of religious pluralism. Ultimately we will have to set any valid theology of the Christian-

---

[48]"Jews and Christians in the World of Tomorrow," *Immanuel* 6 (Spring 1976), 79.

Jewish relationship within such a broader interreligious frame-work.

A theology of religious pluralism might allow us to say that our particular tradition has more insight than others, but no longer can we maintain that it has a lock on all significant religious insight. This does not mean, of course, that each religious tradition is incapable of providing salvation for those who have given it their allegiance in faith. What it does highlight is the recognition that ultimately, until the eschaton, all people are saved in their incompleteness. Further discussion of this point is certainly called for since we are only in the very early stages of the emergence of a theology of religious pluralism in both Christianity and Judaism.

In this context we need to recognize a crucial, more pervasive result of the Christian-Jewish dialogue. The extent to which we as Christians can create positive theological space for the Jewish People against whom we originally forged Christian identity, to that same extent shall we moderate, even if implicitly, all absolutist claims for the Christian faith relative to any other religious tradition. Because the Christian church has so often framed its relationship to Judaism in "over-against" language, far more than has been true for other faiths, any alterations in the theological model of the Christian-Jewish relationship will inevitably re-verberate favorably on its ability to relate to these religions as well. Gerald Anderson, an expert in the study of Christian missionary activity, has rightly concluded that any substantial changes in the Christian theological understanding of Judaism will produce a "domino" effect with respect to the other world religions.[49] In a sense, Anderson is also reaffirming the previously mentioned dictum of the great Protestant thinker Karl Barth who insisted that the Christian-Jewish dialogue was the most funda-mental dialogue of all.

A final point should be added here regarding the reformulation of the theology of the Christian-Jewish relationship. Our efforts will remain incomplete and with only modest effect at best on the

---

[49]"Response to Pietro Rossano," in Gerald H. Anderson and Thomas F. Stransky (eds.), *Christ's Lordship and Religious Pluralism.* NY: Orbis, 1981, 118-119.

general body of the Christian community unless we find ways to incorporate the post-Vatican II consciousness of an ongoing, constructive link between the church and the Jewish People in our liturgical life. Much of the present liturgy, particularly during the central periods of Advent/Christmas and Lent/Easter, focuses on the theme of Jesus as fulfillment of the biblical prophecies regarding the messiah and the inauguration of the messianic era. Yet it is clear from the works of the theologians examined in this chapter that nearly all who have reflected seriously on the Christian-Jewish relationship in light of the Christological proclamation now reject, or at least seriously moderate, the traditional claims of the church in this regard. They then try to find the uniqueness of the Christ Event in areas other than messianic fulfillment. Unless the church confronts this pivotal, though admittedly difficult, issue, the reformulated Christologies about which we have spoken will remain in the realm of pure theory, with hardly any impact on the ordinary Christian believer's outlook towards the Jewish People and their covenantal tradition.

2

Contemporary Christology and Judaism: A Constructive Proposal in the Light of Pharisaic Judaism

I. New Testament Fulfillment Claims

In an address to a Christian-Jewish conference in Philadelphia some years ago the biblical scholar W. D. Davies made a very telling point. He insisted that although the New Testament definitely describes Jesus as the fulfillment of *some* Jewish messianic prophecies it never suggests he fulfilled all such prophecies. This is certainly a valuable insight. It does much to dash the claims of those past and present Christians who would argue that through Jesus Christianity stands as the total fulfillment of Judaism with the clear implication that post-Easter Judaism constitutes nothing but an empty shell.

Davies' statement, however, does still leave us with many unresolved problems. First of all, it places a leading New Testament scholar, and an important contributor to the church's current rethinking of Judaism, on the side of that school of thought which definitely acknowledges fulfillment claims on the part of the gospel writers. This means that we must begin any discussion of Christology and Judaism with the *datum* that our biblical tradition does in fact make the claim, in some parts at least, that the Christ Event brought to completion important dimensions of the promise made to the People Israel, even if that completion was less exhaustive than the church has often portrayed it to be. Acknowledging this fulfillment claim as a starting point, we then are confronted with a second difficulty. How do we deal with it if we wish to create meaningful theological space for Judaism and to underscore the continuing bonds existing between Jews and Christians after the Christ Event in the spirit of recent official Catholic teaching? There are several possibilities. We could fall back on the approach of Romans 9-11 employed by the early pioneers in the Christian-Jewish dialogue and simply say that Judaism does retain theological meaning from the Christian perspective even though we cannot clearly square this assertion with the apparent fulfillment claims in the gospels. Or we could try to isolate those aspects of the Jewish messianic vision that Jesus fulfilled, with some indication of those dimensions of Judaism that still await their crowning glory. These later dimensions would then constitute the *raison d'etre* of Judaism in the common era. While such an approach might have some possibilities, it too is inadequate. It would leave Judaism breathing in light of the Christ Event, but barely so.

Feeling that neither of the two above avenues are satisfactory, and clearly joining with the increasing number of Christian theologians who, as we have seen in chapter one, have rejected excessive Christian claims of total fulfillment in Christ, I am forced to take a position that is somewhat different. It is one that has much in common with several of the double covenantal theologians discussed previously, especially Clemens Thoma and Franz Mussner. I accept as a given the contention that earlier strata of the New Testament picture Jesus as the completion of many of the major messianic claims of the Hebrew Scriptures. Any attempt to promote a new constructive theology of Christian-Jewish relations today that does not first acknowledge and work through this real tension will inevitably fall down. The point I would make, and where I would definitely move beyond W.D. Davies' contention, is that the later parts of the New Testament quietly ease away from some of these fulfillment claims as the basis of Christological statement. This shift is in fact quite subtle, as perforce it had to be. A fragile, still growing movement does not make an abrupt public change without seriously endangering its very existence. The leaders of the early church were surely aware of this sociological reality. More will be said about this issue later in this chapter. It is obvious, however, that the New Testament leaves us with a dilemma. How do we decide between the fulfillment Christology that largely dominates the synoptic gospels and the consciousness Christology, or what Mussner has called the Son Christology, rooted in the Incarnation that appears so prominently in the later Pauline writings and in the gospel of John?

A solution to the above conflict as to which of two fundamental approaches to Christology should serve as the basis for Christian faith expression in our time can come *only,* and I strongly emphasize *only,* if we are willing to grant certain methodological principles in the handling of New Testament materials. The first is the willingness to grant that not all parts of the New Testament have equal value for today. Applied to the problem at hand, this principle will allow us to say that the later consciousness Christology ought to be the starting point for Christological expression today rather than the messianic fulfillment Christology which dominates the synoptics. This principle has been employed by several New Testament scholars, including Raymond Brown who has applied it to certain clearly antisemitic texts in John (such as those which equate Jews with the forces of darkness), which he argues can no longer be proclaimed as authentic kerygma by contemporary Christianity.[1]

The second principle is the assertion that revelation is developmental rather than static and that it continues to exist as the church advances the building of the kingdom in community with the Jewish People through its participation in the flow of human history. This principle allows us to say that consciousness Christology should be the basis of contemporary Christology not only because it seems to be the product of more mature apostolic reflection rather than initial faith enthusiasm but primarily because subsequent history has shown us the unsuitability of any fulfillment claims. This unsuitability is evident both because of

---

[1]Cf. *The Community of the Beloved Disciple.* New York: Paulist, 1979.

the continued presence of evil and suffering, as Rosemary Ruether has pointed out, and because of the tenacious vitality of the People Israel despite events such as the Nazi Holocaust. Unless Christians are prepared to accept a developmental notion of revelation there is little basis for hope in overcoming the dominance of the messianic fulfillment Christology in the churches with the disastrous consequences it has had for our image of Judaism and the concrete relationship with Jews.

II. The Pharisaic Context of Christology

My particular preference for consciousness Christology as found in the later Pauline writings and John should now be clear. To understand this "word-made-flesh" Christology, as J. Coert Rylaarsdam has termed it, there is need to appreciate fully the close links between Jesus and the progressive Pharisaic movement in Second Temple Judaism. Because the Pharisees have been so maligned in Christian education, as both my study of Catholic textbooks as well as Dr. Eugene Fisher's update have demonstrated,[2] it will prove difficult to introduce this connection into the mainstream of Christian thinking. But this is an imperative if we are to make genuine progress on the Christological question. The 1985 Vatican *Notes,* spoken of in chapter one, assisted this process substantially by affirming that Jesus stood closer to Pharisaism than any other Jewish movement of his time. Purifying the image of the Pharisees in Christian teaching becomes important not ony for the sake of removing a source of continuing prejudice against Judaism, but in order to clarify in a positive vein the authentic meaning of the Christ Event.

A few pioneering scholars in the United States such as R. Travers Herford began to cut through Pharisaic stereotypes early on in this century. But it has been only recently that both Christian and Jewish scholars have devoted extensive research to

---

[2]Cf. John T. Pawlikowski, *Cathechetics and Prejudice.* New York: Paulist, 1973 and Eugene J. Fisher, *Faith Without Prejudice.* New York: Paulist, 1977.

this period.[3] Though they are far from unanimous in their conclusions and disagree regarding the reliability of certain ancient sources such as historian Josephus, a general trend is slowly emerging which is revolutionary in terms of the classical Christian understanding of the movement as the arch-enemies of Jesus, as a group diametrically opposed to his basic teachings. This new appreciation of the Pharisaic movement is also proving to have deep implications for the church's Christological interpretation. For as Christian scholars continue to examine the fundamental outlook of Pharisaism, the more striking the parallels with the gospel portraits of Jesus become. This is not to say that Pharisaism was a rigid movement with tightly prescribed beliefs. It had many subgroups who often heatedly disagreed with one another. Jesus seems closest to the Pharisaic viewpoint associated with the great Rabbi Hillel, in which God's love was a predominant motif. But whatever their differences on particular points, all these Pharisaic schools shared an overall common orientation that clearly set them apart from the religious-political outlook of their chief rivals of the period, the Sadducees.

For many people in the church, equating Jesus with the Pharisaic movement to any degree will sound blasphemous. After all the gospels appear on the surface to present a uniformly

---

[3]Scholarship on Pharisaism includes: R. Travers Herford, *The Pharisees*. Boston: Beacon, 1962; Louis Finkelstein, *The Pharisees,* 2 vols. Philadelphia: Jewish Publication Society, 1962; Asher Finkel, *The Pharisees and the Teacher of Nazareth.* Leiden, Holland: Brill, 1964; William E. Phipps, "Jesus, the Prophetic Pharisee," *Journal of Ecumenical Studies,* 14:1 (Winter 1977), 17-31; Clemens Thoma, *A Christian Theology,* chapters 3 and 4; Ellis Rivkin, *A Hidden Revolution: The Pharisees' Search for the Kingdom Within.* Nashville: Abingdon, 1978 and "Defining the Pharisees: The Tannaitic Sources," *Hebrew Union College Annual* 1970, 205-249; Jacob Neusner, *The Rabbinic Traditions About the Pharisees Before 70,* 3 vols. Leiden, Holland: Brill, 1971, *From Politics to Piety: The Emergence of Pharisaic Judaism.* Englewood Cliffs, NJ: Prentice-Hall, 1973 and "The Use of the Later Rabbinc Evidence for the Study of First-Century Pharisaism," in *Approaches to Ancient Judaism: Theory and Practice,* edited by William Scott Green, Brown Judaic Studies 1. Missoula, MT: Scholar's Press, 1978.; John Bowker, *Jesus and the Pharisees.* London: Cambridge University Press, 1973; Michael Cook, "Jesus and the Pharisees—the Problem as It Stands Today," *Journal of Ecumenical Studies,* 15:3 (Summer 1978), 441-460; Philip Culbertson, "Changing Images of the Pharisees," *Anglican Theological Review,* 64, 359-61; Stuart E. Rosenberg, *The Christian Problem: A Jewish View,* chapter 8. New York: Hippocrene, 1986; Leonard Swidler, "The Pharisees in Recent Catholic Writing," Horizons, 10:2 (Fall 1983), 267-287.

negative image of the movement. Recent biblical interpretation, however, makes us suspect that this "apparent" surface picture may in fact not be the full story, especially as we come to know better the actual beliefs of the Pharisees. We must be cautious here. It is entirely possible, indeed very likely, that we will never be able to know precisely the relationship between Jesus and this movement. The requisite sources are not there and the extant ones are ambiguous in many areas and in some cases may reflect a pro-Pharisaic bias that has resulted in a somewhat exalted description of the group's ideals and successes. That is why the statement of the Vatican *Notes,* which refrains from clearly linking Jesus with the movement while affirming a definite congruency of perspective on certain key issues, may represent as far as sound scholarship will ever take us with respect to this question. Recent indications, however, that there were five to seven major Pharisaic subgroups which often employed bitter language in reference to one another (as the Talmud shows us to some extent), that the most vitriolic denunciations of Pharisaism occur in the later gospel of Matthew in contrast to the earlier Marcan version and hence may reflect concrete tensions between church and synagogue subsequent to Jesus' time, and that the term "Pharisee" may be used far more selectively than we once thought have led contemporary Catholicism to the conclusion that the image of the Pharisees and their relationship to Jesus needs to be redrawn.[4]

A careful examination of the extant sources regarding the Pharisees shows us that their movement signaled a profound theological reorientation in Judaism in nothing less than the basic God-humanity relationship. For the Pharisaic movement the God of Revelation now assumed the role of the Father of each individual person. No longer was God seen only as the parent of the patriarchs, as intimate only with a select group of priests, prophets and kings in Israel. The God of Abraham, Isaac and Sarah now related in a profoundly intimate way to each and every individual, whatever their particular status in the society. There were no longer gradations of divine intimacy in principle.

---

[4] Cf. "Defining the Pharisees."

Each person acquired the right in this Pharisaic perspective to address God directly as Father. Though the Pharisees worked somewhat subtly, they eventually succeeded in a fundamental reshaping of Jewish society, helped in their effort by the destruction of the Temple in the war with Rome. A leading contemporary scholar of Pharisaism, Ellis Rivkin, describes the basic Pharisaic vision in this way:

> When we ask ourselves the source of this generative power we find it in the relationship the Pharisees established between the One God and the singular individual. The Father God cared about *you;*He was concerned about *you.* He watched over *you;* He loved *you;* and loved *you* so much that He wished *your* unique self to live forever.... The Heavenly Father was ever present. One could talk to Him, plead with Him, cry out to Him, pray to Him—person to Person, individual to Individual, heart to Heart, soul to Soul. It was the establishment of this personal relationship, an inner experience, that accounts for the manifest power of Pharisaism to live on.[5]

It should be noted at this point in light of present-day theological concerns that the clear association of God and the Father image may indeed have had a shadow side. It did mark the first time that Israel's God was so explicitly described in male imagery. Intended or not, this may have strengthened the patriarchal system which many find the root cause of most of the social ills in today's world. This issue should be pursued. But in so doing we should not lose sight of the genuinely positive contributions resulting from the Pharisaic understanding of God as Father. Certainly the basic dignity conferred on all people through this divine imagery should in principle help to destroy the evils associated with patriarchy whether or not the initial framers of the Pharisaic vision fully recognized this or not. It is not the Pharisaic "Father" notion that created patriarchy. It is also quite

[5]*A Hidden Revolution,* 310.

legitimate to hold out the belief that we ought to move away from this imagery in our day. But we should not do so until we have fully appropriated its fundamental vision of human equality.

The Pharisees' sense of God as Father and the personal intimacy it involved was so intense that they felt obligated to create new divine names. Older terms for God from the Hebrew Scriptures were used only when they actually quoted the sacred texts. Among their principal names for God, in addition to the fundamental one of Father, were *Makom,* "the all present," *Skekhinah,* "the divine presence"; *Ha-Kadosh Baruch Hu,* "The Holy One Blessed Be He"; and *Mi She-Amar Ve-Hayah Olam,* "He who spoke and the world came into being." There is little question that these fresh divine terms reflected the importance attached by Pharisaism to its perception of a newly understood depth in the God-humanity relationship. A profound change in human self-understanding was in process and the Pharisees were struggling for adequate verbal symbols through which to express the new revelation that they had grasped.

Associating the Pharisees with Jesus in any positive way will still strike many Christians as strange, if not totally unfaithful, to the witness of the Synoptic gospels. For their surface portrayal in these books appears as anything but complimentary. We do have to acknowledge that there is a problem here for any viewpoint espousing a close connection between Jesus and Pharisaism. And it is not one capable of simple resolution. Partly this is due to our inability to separate clearly the actual teachings of Jesus from those of the later church (where the hostility against the Pharisees may have been more intense) and to ascertain the precise outlooks of the Pharisees of Jesus' time, since our records for the period were edited at a much later date and may far more reflect Pharisaic beliefs subsequent to Jesus' death. Nonetheless there are several tentative ways of resolving this difficulty that show some possibilities.

The first suggestion was advanced some years ago by James Parkes. He contrasted the image of the Pharisees in the earlier gospel of Mark with that found in the later Matthew. In Mark the Jesus/Pharisaic relationship appears reserved and generally respectful while in Matthew it is marked by continual hostility and conflict. The Marcan narrative does not establish a definite break between Jesus and the Pharisees until the incident when Jesus permits his disciples to pluck corn on the Sabbath and then proceeds to heal the man with the withered arm, using the Pharisaic principle "the Sabbath was made for man, not man for the Sabbath" as the justification. These actions did turn a relationship of "reserved interest" into one of heightened opposition in Mark, but still devoid of Matthew's frequently vitriolic language. But even this later opposition in Mark, according to Parkes, can be interpreted somewhat positively if we understand it within the complex political and social setting of the period, in which the very survival of the Jewish people was threatened by the Jewish Hellenists' call for assimilation into Roman society. Protecting the observance of the Sabbath was seen by the Pharisees in this context as a vital means of Jewish communal preservation.

For Parkes, then, the opposition between Jesus and the Pharisees is rooted in a conflict of two principles both of which are valid in their own right. Jesus chose to emphasize the total dignity of each individual person, the Pharisees the significance of maintaining group identity. Parkes insists that both Jesus and the Pharisees were right in retrospect. While they took their stand on different aspects of the human situation, both the realities—the inviolable dignity of each human person and the inherent communitarian dimension of human life—to which they separately bore witness are crucial for any complete understanding of humanity. Neither in the end told us how to resolve this ongoing tension still facing humankind.

With this approach to the relatively mild Marcan tension between Jesus and the Pharisees, Parkes saw the much more severe opposition in Matthew as coming from the period after Jesus' death. It reflected far more the hostilities between the nascent church and the synagogue after the formal expulsion of Christians as each group struggled for converts and a new identity in the first century of the common era.

The second proposed explanation of the Jesus/Pharisees conflict takes its cue from the Talmud. There we find reference to seven different types of Pharisees. Five of these groups draw a negative judgment in materials that are basically of Pharisaic/ rabbinic origin. Awareness of this Talmudic condemnation of certain Pharisaic groups opens the door for the proposal that what we have in the gospel such as Matthew is not a global condemnation of *the* Pharisees, but a selective attack by Jesus in the Talmudic manner on those Pharisaic groups that were opposing him within the framework of the general movement. This viewpoint gains some support from the research of Ellis Rivkin, who has found that the name "Pharisee" was considered pejorative by the Pharisees themselves. They opted to call themselves scribes or the wise ones.[6] The Pharisees' chief antagonists of the time, the Sadducees, clearly employed this term in attacking them. The members of the movement in turn may well have made use of a term originally conceived as an indictment of them by the Sadducees against those within the brotherhood whom they felt were deviating from authentic Pharisaic ideals, as a way of heaping additional derision on them. Matthew's gospel may reflect Jesus' active participation in this effort. Put another way, "the Pharisees" denounced by Jesus may in fact have been people within the movement whom he and other Hillel-oriented Pharisees, who made divine love a core element of their proclamation, viewed as destructive for the future of the Jewish People and its covenantal relationship with God.

At this moment, we need to pursue both these possible explanations somewhat further. We may never be able to determine the exact Jesus/Pharisaic relationship with full scholarly certainty. But, based on what we have been able to learn about the central teachings of Pharisaism as a whole in the last decade of research in particular, and recognizing the close parallels between so many of these teachings and the basic message of Jesus, we have every reason to bring into play what David Tracy has called "the hermeneutic of suspicion" with reference to the apparent wholesale opposition between Jesus and Pharisaism which emerges from a first reading of the Synoptic gospels.

[6]"Defining the Pharisees," 240-41.

III. Jesus and the Pharisees: A Shared Vision

It would now be useful to turn to some of these actual parallels between Pharisaic thought and that of Jesus, parallels which, as Michael Cook has remarked, more than any other evidence undercut the picture of total "overagainstness" found in many parts of the gospels.[7]

The Pharisees were convinced that a major overhaul of Jewish society and of the Jewish approach to religious expression was in order as a result of their new perception of the intimacy of the God-humanity relationship. This included: (1) moving the notion of "oral Torah," of ongoing interpretation of the "written Torah" to a central place in religious understanding, according this "oral Torah" the same Mosaic authority as the biblical books themselves: (2) developing the position of the rabbi, a new lay leader and teacher, whose authority came in virtue of performance and service not blood line (as with the priests) and who gradually assumed a prominence previously reserved exclusively for the temple priests; (3) the creation of the synagogue as a rival institution to the Temple, an institution where a high measure of equality prevailed and which was seen as the center of Jewish communal responsibility; (4) the centering of ordinary liturgical life around table-fellowship where all could participate rather than the exclusively priestly sacrificial cult at the Temple; and (5) the notion of resurrection, but only after the end-time had arrived. The Sadducees attacked this last Pharisaic doctrine with particular vehemence.

A careful scrutiny of the ministry and teachings of Jesus in the New Testament gives good evidence of similar patterns and concerns. There are any number of instances where Jesus is clearly using the process of "oral Torah" as he reinterprets the Hebrew Scriptures according to the circumstances prevailing in the Palestine of his day. And the abiding emphasis in his ministry on teaching and healing clearly fits the pattern the Pharisaic movement set for a rabbi. And although Jesus left no fully

---

[7]"Jesus and the Pharisees," 457.

elaborated view of "church" for his disciples to follow after his death, the example of the early Jerusalem community as depicted in Acts certainly reflects in broad outlines the vision of the synagogue articulated within Pharisaism. Jesus also appears to have been a participant in Pharisaic-type fellowship meals. In fact, there are some good reasons for suspecting that the Christian Eucharist was instituted in just such a setting.

The resemblances continue in the doctrinal realm. Stress on love, on the centrality of the Shemah—the great affirmation of divine unity, on the themes the New Testament collapses into the Beatitudes and on the Resurrection, which certainly became central to later interpretations of the meaning of Jesus' ministry and person, bear witness to the presence of a firm Pharisaic spirit in the message of Jesus. In particular his continual reference to the intimate link he enjoyed with the Father as the mark of his personal identity certainly picks up on the most fundamental of Pharisaic theological themes. Granted that Jesus' awareness of his link with the Father, as both Clemens Thoma and Franz Mussner have correctly insisted, involves a degree of intimacy that the Pharisees were not prepared to grant to any person, nonetheless it draws deeply on the new perception of the God-human relationship that is such a characteristic mark of the movement.

The more we continue to study the basic teachings of Jesus and the outlook of apostolic Christianity in the context of an enhanced understanding of the Pharisaic revolution the more we are struck by fundamental similarities. It is highly unlikely that sufficient documents will ever become available to us to reconstruct the precise links. But we know enough now to realize that we cannot begin to understand the meaning of the Christ Event today without a thorough acquaintance with the Pharisaic movement which provided its indispensable seedbed.

IV. Jesus and the Pharisees: Their Basic Differences

Having indicated, however briefly, the general areas where we find a high degree of influence on Jesus' teachings, we need now to turn to some of the major differences. The first is one to which we have already alluded: the degree of possible divine-human intimacy. On many occasions Jesus uses language which establishes an eternal bonding between himself and the Father which no one else shares in the same way but whose effects redound positively upon all of humanity. The consciousness of a profound divine-human nexus was clearly present in Pharisaism. But notions of separation, of distance (a traditional Jewish sense), remained firm and unbending in the mind even of the most advanced sectors of the Pharisaic movement. This sense of divine-human intimacy on the part of Jesus had some practical consequences for the power of the human community as we shall see shortly.

The second difference has to do with Jesus' attempt to carry the Pharisaic notion of the basic dignity of each human person to its ultimate conclusion. While the Pharisaic notion of God's intimate link with every human being bestowed an inherent value on every life and a certain sense of fundamental equality, the movement was likewise concerned about the realities of the sociopolitical context in which they lived. This concern was shared by all the disparate Pharisaic groups despite their profound internal disagreements. The Pharisees gradually began to view Jesus' uncompromising commitment to the worth of the individual person as a streak of independence that posed a potentially grave threat to Jewish communal survival. Confronted with the threat of Judaism's absorption by Hellenism they devised a plan of Torah observance that included erecting a "fence," as it were, around the Sabbath. Strict faithfulness to the Sabbath precepts became critical for Pharisaism in the battle to preserve the distinctive communal identity and religious mission of the Jewish People. Jesus, on the other hand, showed he was prepared to ignore this fence in cases where human dignity was at stake, though he seems never to have questioned the basic validity of this fence. He attempted to justify his action when challenged by the Pharisees on the basis of a principle highly honored in their tradition: the Sabbath was made for the human person and not vice-versa. The Pharisees had judged this principle too dangerous for the particular time period in which they lived. Jesus thought otherwise. The popularity of Jesus in some quarters raised the threat to national loyalty to Torah which the provisions for strict Sabbath observance were intended to protect.

James Parkes, who wrote extensively on this conflict over Sabbath observance between Jesus and the Pharisaic movement as a crucial factor in whatever degree of tension actually existed between them, made the point that it is essential for contemporary Christians to realize that in this conflict the Pharisees could no more have simply acquiesced to the position advanced by Jesus than he could have accepted theirs. The starting points of each were quite different. Jesus' healing of a diseased hand on the Sabbath, for example, was not in itself the critical issue. The man appeared in no imminent danger of death as a result of his malady. If he were, the Pharisees would have had little objection to the compassionate act of healing on the part of Jesus. He chose not to wait another day when there would have been no problem whatsoever in doing so because, in Parkes' view, he wished to assert "the primacy of each man as person."[8]

Parkes goes on to add that Jesus never tried to bridge the gap between his own vision and the understandable Pharisaic preoccupation with communal preservation:

> Within the divinely chosen community he proclaimed the divine concern with each man as person. It is for men to hold the two in a continuously destroyed and continuously recreated balance. Jesus did not attempt to resolve the tension for us. He challenged us only to recognize that it existed.[9]

Thus, while the Pharisees pushed the concept of each individual's worth a tremendous distance, Jesus stretched it to its final limits. But it needs to be remembered that he did this with the consciousness that the notion of community was already a strong part of the tradition of the people whom he was addressing. Maintaining the proper balance in the ongoing community/individual dialectic is a task he left for us. Too often, however, the

---

[8] *The Theological Foundations,* 177.
[9] *Ibid.*

Christian churches have overemphasized the individual dimension at the expense of the communal. Jesus was willing to push the dignity of the individual and its practical implications beyond the prevailing Pharisaic consensus. But it is hard to imagine, given his deep immersion in the spirit of the People Israel, that he ever intended this highlighting of the individual's inherent worth to erode the strong communal orientation which marks the Hebrew Scriptures. This is definitely an area where Jesus' teaching, when separated from his deep ties with the Jewish tradition, can become highly distorted.

Another possible distinction between Jesus and the Pharisees concerns their respective attitudes toward the *Am Ha Aretz,* the people of the land. Many writers have depicted Jesus as the determined champion of this outcast group, a position that supposedly put him into immediate conflict with the Pharisees who, it is claimed, look upon them with great disdain. There is little doubt on the basis of available New Testament data that Jesus had a persistent interest in the welfare of the *Am Ha Aretz* along with many other "outcast" groups in the society of his time. Such affirmation of the outcast is a pervasive feature of his entire public ministry. What is not really as certain, however, is the claim that this put him totally out of step with the entire Pharisaic movement. Much will depend on what scholarly interpretation of Pharisaism at the time of Jesus one accepts as normative. The research undertaken by Ellis Rivkin and Michael Cook, for example, leads them to the conclusion, in Cook's words, that "the presumed antipathy between the Pharisees and the 'Am Ha Aretz' is not easily demonstrable."[10] Jacob Neusner's basic thesis, found in most of his major writings in the area, that the Pharisees in the time of Jesus had become a somewhat closed table fellowship might tend, on the other hand, to validate the claim of a marked contrast between Jesus and the movement on the *Am Ha Aretz* question, even though Neusner himself does not specifically address the issue.

---

[10]Cf. Ellis Rivkin, "Defining the Pharisees," 205-249 and Michael Cook, "Jesus and the Pharisees," 449.

It is obvious that further research is needed on this question. At the moment, all we can say is that there seems to be something in the contrast between Jesus and the Pharisees, at least in terms of centrality of concern, though all exaggerated claims should be studiously avoided. In line with his demonstrated commitment to the inviolable dignity of each human person, Jesus seemed on the whole more ready to welcome the *Am Ha Aretz* into the company of his disciples and perhaps into his table fellowship than was the case for the Pharisees.

A fourth distinction between Jesus and the Pharisees emerges from the research of Professors David Flusser and Shuel Safrai.[11] They explain that Jesus seized upon a rather popular rabbinic text about a person's inability to serve two masters simultaneously and subtly altered it. For both rabbis and Jesus the first master was God. The difference came in the designation of the second master. In the Pharisaic text it was "evil inclination," which may have had sexual connotations. Jesus dropped this reference (perhaps under Essene influence) and substituted wealth (or mammon) in its place. Thus in Jesus' perspective riches became the antithesis of authentic commitment to God. Riches tended to drive a person away from God because in the process of acquiring wealth people are prone to act in a way that disregards the basic dignity of men and women, which his ministry was continually reaffirming. Once again we see how pivotal this sense of human dignity was in Jesus' proclamation of the Word and the Way.

David Flusser is also an important source for our appreciation of yet another probably unique dimension of Jesus' teaching in comparison to Pharisaism: the love of one's enemy. Following through on his emphasis on the fundamental dignity inherent in each person, Jesus urged upon his followers a positive attitude of respect and love even for those who had harmed them in some fashion. New Testament scholar Donald Senior makes much the same point as Flusser regarding the totally umcompromising nature of love in Jesus' message, which extends even to the

---

[11]"The Slave of Two Masters," *Immanuel* 6 (Spring 1976), 30-33.

enemy.[12] Flusser sums up Jesus' stance in the following words:

> It is clear that Jesus' moral approach to God and man . . . is unique and incomparable. According to the teachings of Jesus you have to love the sinners, while according to Judaism you have not to hate the wicked. It is important to note that the positive love even toward the enemies is Jesus' personal message. We do not find this doctrine in the New Testament outside of the words of Jesus himself. . . . In Judaism hatred is practically forbidden. But love to the enemy is not prescribed.[13]

Here we have another instance of the dignity of the individual person assuming a primacy for Jesus that takes him beyond the parameters of the Pharisaic movement. As on several other key issues, Jesus pushed a fundamental Pharisaic outlook to its outer limits.

Clemens Thoma has brought to the surface what appears to be a sixth point of contrast between Jesus and the Pharisees. Once more, however, it is a question of a degree rather than absolute difference. On the basis of his research into the New Testament in the light of his extensive understanding of the rabbinic materials, Thoma has concluded that Jesus preached the actual presence of the reign of God in his activities and person to an extent that alienated him from Pharisaism despite his otherwise intimate ties to the movement. While Thoma rejects the classical Christian contention of the kingdom or reign of God being *fully* present in Jesus and posits the full reconciliation of God and the human community as a still future event, it was not *all future* for Jesus as the Pharisees seemed to assume. While great care must be taken in how this difference is stated, lest we fall back into the old Messianic-fulfillment Christologies which Thoma has rightly

Donald Senior, C.P. (eds.), *Biblical and Theological Reflections on the Challenge of Peace*, 55-72.

[12]Cf. "Enemy Love: The Challenge of Peace," *The Bible Today*, 21:3 (May 1983), 163-169 and "Jesus' Most Scandalous Teaching," in John T. Pawlikowski, O. S. M. and

[13]"A New Sensitivity in Judaism and the Christian Message," *Harvard Theological Review*, 61:2 (April 1968), 126.

rejected, there does seem to be some basis for differentiating the stances of Jesus and the Pharisees along these lines.[14]

Another point of contrast relates to the forgiveness of sin. Despite their willingness to modify earlier Jewish views in many areas, the Pharisees continued to hold tenaciously to the traditional view in this area: God alone possessed the power and authority to forgive sins. In the gospels we see Jesus laying claim to this power for himself. This is of course something less than surprising given his overall consciousness of a unique bonding with the Father. But he does more than this. It is here that the practical, pastoral side of the new "God-as-Father" theology comes to the fore. Jesus transfers the power to forgive sins from himself to those disciples who have accepted his word. This is indeed a revolutionary move within that milieu. It represented a powerful statement about the intimacy now possible between humanity and divinity because of Jesus' unique sonship. God stands willing to share with the human community one of the most treasured of divine prerogatives—the power to forgive and reconcile. While the Pharisees strongly emphasized the new intimacy between God and people of which they had become profoundly conscious, they were clearly unwilling to admit that the human/divine bond could ever assume such total interpenetration, that the sharing relationship could become so deep. This transfer of the previously exclusive divine power of reconciliation to his disciples represented on Jesus' part a further affirmation of the basic dignity of the human person around which his ministry so prominently turned.

Another important element in Jesus' distinctiveness vis-a-vis the overall Pharisaic movement involves his basic political stance. He seems to have been more willing to confront the political status quo in his day at the intermediate level of power—the Temple in Jerusalem, though for whatever reasons he joined the mainline Pharisees in walking a rather fine line regarding ultimate Roman authority. He was not a Zealot as scholars such as S.G.F. Brandon have claimed, though he may have been put to death as

---

[14]Cf. Clemens Thoma, *A Christian Theology*, 113-115.

one by the imperial authorities.[15] But neither was he merely an itinerant preacher of peace who fundamentally spoke words of internal conversion rather than words of direct and immediate political challenge, as Oscar Cullmann and the U.S. Bishops' Peace Pastoral make him out to be.[16]

An understanding of the Pharisaic viewpoint which had a profound impact on Jesus enables us to see that there were avenues for political action in the period other than the Zealots. When we drop the false equation of political equals Zealot in Jesus' day and acknowledge the pervasive Pharisaic challenge to the authority of the Jerusalem Temple which was as much the center of local political power in Palestine as of religious authority, we can more quickly recognize the activist political dimensions of Jesus' ministry. We do not have to posit, as Brandon did, some pre-gospel documents that were politically neutralized by the evangelists for fear the fledging apostolic community would be endangered if Rome should discover the complete message of its founder. Read with a Pharisaic eye, the gospels present ample evidence of a political Jesus.

The most important episode by far is Jesus' invasion of the Temple to drive out the moneychangers. Classically this incident has been described as a protest against cultic impurity. No doubt this is true in part. But there is far greater significance to this dramatic act. Properly placed in the context of the period, the invasion represents direct confrontation of the total Temple system which both Jesus and the Pharisees found deficient. Their opposition had a twofold origin. They were upset at the concrete abuses in the fiscal area that had reportedly penetrated the system up to the high priests themselves. Official corruption seemed rife. But even more importantly they objected to the very basis of the Temple system, one built around an elite class of priests who inherited power merely on the basis of their bloodline. Such a

---

[15]*Jesus and the Zealots* . New York: Charles Scribner's 1967. Also cf. special issue of *Judaism* on this topic, 20:1 (Winter 1971).

[16]Cf. Oscar Cullmann, *Jesus and the Revolutionaries.* New York: Harper & Row, 1970 and my chapter, "Power and the Pursuit of Peace: Some Reflections," in John T. Pawlikowski, O.S.M. and Donald Senior, C.P., *Biblical and Theological Reflections,* 73-89.

system in their judgment inevitably breeds injustice.

In the present gospel narratives, the invasion occurs immediately prior to Jesus' passion and death. In fact the incident may have taken place at the outset of Jesus' public ministry, bringing him a degree of notoriety.[17] By placing it where they did, however, the evangelists transformed it into a kind of "culminating" pericope. It served as a terse yet powerful summation of Jesus' three years of public ministry. In a volume titled *Jesus Before Christianity: The Gospel of Liberation*, the South African theologian Albert Nolan, O.P. explicitly rejects any notion that sees the Temple invasion merely as a protest against empty ritual. Jesus' concern, says Nolan, "was not to gain power or to purify ritual. His concern was *the abuse of money and trade,* "[18] Ample evidence exists in his judgment that the Temple moneychangers took advantage of the demand for clean animals for sacrifice by charging exorbitant rates, with some of the excessive profits likely finding their way into the hands of the priests. Jesus was determined to confront this exploitation. According to Nolan, "his compassion for the poor and the oppressed overflowed once more into indignation and anger."[19]

Nolan's analysis of the Temple invasion remains inadequate in at least one major respect. He fails to bring out clearly enough that Jesus' concern about the oppression of the poor by the moneychangers was not an isolated criticism of Temple activities but amounted to a fundamental challenge to the entire religious-political system that the Temple embodied. It was the whole style of worship and the privileged status of the priests with its inherited power that generated the concrete abuses in the selling of sacrificial animals. In Jesus' mind it was not enough to stop these specific acts. The whole temple system had to go.

The conclusion from the New Testament evidence is therefore that Jesus was a political activist who did not stop short of directly attacking the immediate power center in his society. He did so as

---

[17]Cf. Etienne Trocmé, "L'Expulsion des Marchands du Tempe," *New Testament Studies,* 15 (1968/69), 1-22.

[18]Capetown, RSA: David Philip. 1977.

[19]*Ibid.,* 102.

part of his fundamental proclamation of human dignity. While he was acting on a Pharisaic impulse and out of a Pharisaic heart, most of the Pharisees probably saw the invasion as far too dangerous a move at the time in terms of the welfare of the Jewish community. They preferred to undermine the exclusive authority and power of the Temple priesthood in far more subtle ways. Because of the enhanced status of every individual person which his "sonship" relationship with the Father had made possible, Jesus could no longer go along with such abuses for a time in the hope of effecting gradual change from the bottom up. Jesus fully recognized that the new consciousness of intimacy with the Father-God had profound ramifications for fundamental social organization. An entirely new social model was necessary. The Pharisees saw this in the main as well. But Jesus was determined to start work on this reconstruction immediately, whatever the costs in terms of tension with Rome.

The final example of a distinguishing mark in Jesus' preaching which brought strong Pharisaic opposition has to do with his position towards the Law or to use the Hebrew term that is far richer, the Torah. It is one of the most central issues in the relationship between Jesus and the Pharisees and hence also in any projected theological model for the Jewish-Christian relationship today. But without doubt it remains one of the most elusive as well, with firm conclusions not yet available. We are admittedly in a period of transition on this vital issue within the world of scholarship. For a long time Jesus was frequently portrayed in popular preaching and in Protestant theologies in particular as the person whose coming totally abrogated the Jewish Torah and inaugurated a new sense of freedom. In recent years this theme has been developed anew by many liberation theologians[20] and some feminist theologians.[21]

The last decade has witnessed a remarkable flowering of new

---

[20]Cf. my volume *Christ in the Light of the Christian-Jewish Dialogue.* New York/ Ramsey: Paulist Press, 1982, 59-75.

[21]Cf. Deborah McCauley and Annette Daum, "Jewish-Christian Feminist Dialogue, A Wholistic Vision," *Union Seminary Quarterly Review,* 38:2 (1983), 147-190.

scholarly inquiry into the Jewishness of Jesus.[22] This has in turn called into serious question Jesus' supposed total opposition and abrogation of the Law, which has served as the centerpiece of so much of the church's theology and preaching. Krister Stendahl in a groundbreaking piece titled "The Apostle Paul and the Introspective Conscience of the West"[23] argued that Western Christians have imposed upon Pauline writings, the source for much of the "freedom" interpretation of Jesus' message, a mindset rooted far more in Luther's personal struggles with sin than with Paul's fundamental attitudes or Jesus' actual teachings. In so doing they have intensified the Jewish-Christian problem. And a Catholic biblical scholar Fr. Gerard Sloyan in a study called *Is Christ the End of the Law*[24] concluded that Jesus in no way abrogated the Torah but only brought to completion some of its key dimensions.

Recently, E. P. Sanders, whose writings have made a significant contribution to the process some have described as the contemporary "re-Judaization" of Christianity, has offered a comprehensive review of present-day scholarship and some tentative conclusions.[25] The conclusions may be summarized as follows: Other than the demand to the man whose father had died, we see no instances in the New Testament of where Jesus transgressed the Torah. On the contrary, he seems to have followed it quite precisely and defended its observance against those extreme elements in Palestinian Judaism that were urging total assimilation into the Hellenistic culture. Nor would he countenance a cavalier attitude on the part of others toward the Law. "We find no criticism of the law," says Sanders, "which would allow us to speak of his opposing or rejecting it."[26]

What placed Jesus in tension with the Pharisaic movement on the question of Torah observance was their seeming belief that

[22]For a brief overview, cf. Robin Scroggs, "The Judaizing of the New Testament," *The Chicago Theological Seminary Register*, LXXXVI:1 (Winter 1986), 36-45.

[23]Cf. *Harvard Theological Review*, 56 (July 1963).

[24]Philadelphia: Westminster, 1978.

[25]Cf. *Jesus and Judaism*, Philadelphia: Fortress, 1985, 245-269. Also cf. *Paul and Palestinian Judaism*. Philadelphia: Fortress, 1977 and *Paul, The Law, and the Jewish People*. Philadelphia: Fortress, 1983.

[26]*Jesus and Judaism*, 269.

the Mosaic dispensation was "final or absolutely binding."[27] For Jesus Torah was not final. His sense of the immediacy of the Father God's presence led him to the conviction that the kingdom, though still future, was somehow being inaugurated in his midst. This brings us back to the point that Clemens Thoma so strongly emphasized about proximity of God's reign in Jesus' consciousness. Sanders himself puts it this way: "It was Jesus' sense of living at the turn of the ages which allowed him to think that Mosaic law was not final and absolute."[28] Such thinking on Jesus' part generated tension between himself and Pharisaism that was not easily resolvable.

V. The Shift Towards Christology

Having tried to highlight, albeit in capsule form, the apparent similarities and differences between Jesus and the Pharisaic movement we need now to turn our attention to the shift to Christology. As the early church began to reflect on the significance of Jesus' ministry and the witness to personal contact with him, how was the continuing relationship with Judaism to be interpreted? Rosemary Ruether has charged, for example, that anti-Judaism became Christology's "left-hand".

The development of the earliest New Testament Christologies remains a difficult puzzle to piece together. There is lack of scholarly consensus on many critical points due in no small measure to the paucity of authentic documentation. Considerable work has been done, for example, in trying to pinpoint the meaning of the various titles attributed to Jesus. But some contemporary theologians see this as essentially a dead end and do not put much weight on the significance of particular titles such as "son of man" or "son of David." They prefer to concentrate on the reality underlying these titles, all of which constituted imperfect expressions of this reality.

[27] *Ibid.*
[28] *Ibid.*, 267.

At the heart of this underlying reality is the notion of the Incarnation, the Word made flesh. After reflection on Jesus' teaching and ministry and through continued contact with his presence through sacrament, the early church reached a deeper understanding of a new level of intimacy in the continuing link between humanity and divinity. As Christian faith spread in cultures dominated by a Greek rather than a Hebraic mode of thought, the need arose for a more formalized expression of this experience of Jesus, who had now become the Christ living on in the Christian community's midst in the presence of his Spirit. Thus was Christology born.

The actual development of a Christology, or to be more accurate several versions of Christology, appears to have followed this general path. After an initial interpretation of Jesus as the one promised by the Jewish Messianic tradition, a perspective that is clearly dominant in the earliest strata of the gospel materials and the first of the Pauline writings, difficulties arose for the leaders of the early church. The problems which beset them threatened to sabotage the faith of the fledgling community. It was becoming rather evident that the signs and realities which the prophets had associated with the appearance of the Messiah were nowhere to be seen. The later Pauline writings and the fourth gospel tried to respond to this genuine faith challenge by re-examining the initial Christological statements.

Central to this second attempt at Christological formulation is a shift away from viewing Jesus as the fulfillment of Messianic prophecies towards understanding the revelation of the Christ Event as the unfolding of a linkage between God and humanity far deeper than anyone ever thought possible. If we are to believe the research undertaken by Fr. Raymond Brown, and I think we must, this development had some liturgical origins. The proclamation of God-becoming-human person as the core revelation of the Christ Event was a realization that grew slowly. Brown contends that there exists relative silence about the divine dimensions of Jesus in the earliest strata of the New Testament. The earliest examples of the church applying the title "God" to Jesus (and thus shifting the focus away from Jesus as Messiah) all come from the liturgically-based New Testament passages. Nowhere do the gospels or epistles use the title "God" in a direct fashion relative to the Jesus of ministry.[29]

It was only after in-depth reflection on the meaning of the Christ Event combined with the experience of God's presence in the liturgy that the early church had sufficient insight to understand fully what Jesus had revealed. And even then they recognized that the crucial aspect of this revelation was the intimate link between God and humanity that remains after the Death/ Resurrection of Jesus and in which the human community can participate in some measure. Hence they limited use of the term "God" for those moments when they were essentially speaking of Christ as a theological expression of this ongoing divine-human bond rather than the person Jesus whose life on earth made this visible to humankind. In the Johannine literature it is only the pre-existent Word or the Son in the Father's presence or the resurrected Jesus who is hailed as God. And the doxologies common to Pauline writings acknowledge as God only the triumphant Jesus. In the epistle to the Hebrews the stress is on the Jesus whose throne is forever.

With the research of Fr. Brown as background for the notion of a developmental Christology in the early church culminating in the Incarnation, we can now try to state briefly the positive meaning of this new revelation. Put as simply as possible, what the church finally understood with far greater clarity through the person and ministry of Jesus, including his Death/Resurrection, was how profoundly integral humanity was to the self-definition of God. This new consciousness also led to the consequent realization that if humanity is integral to God, then humankind must also share in some way in what we call divinity. Each human person is somehow divine, he or she somehow shares in the constitutive nature of God. Christ becomes the principal theological symbol in Christianity for expressing this basic reality. As scholars have discovered from an examination of the later strata of New Testament sources, this humanity existed in the Godhead from the very beginning. So from one perspective it is quite

[29]Cf. Does the New Testament Call Jesus God?"

true to state that God did not suddenly taken on human form in the person of Jesus. Rather, a measure of humanity always was part of the divine identity. Humanity was integral to the full nature of God. Seen in this light the Christ Event becomes the crucial point at which this "human" reality of God and the bonding it implies first became clearly visible to humankind.

A cautionary remark is in order, however, if the above statements about the eternal divine-human linkage are not to be misrepresented. Nothing said above implies that God is to be equated with the totality of humanity. A gulf continues to persist between God and humankind that remains forever impassable. Moreover, the human community remains aware that despite the profound bonding with God revealed through the Christ Event this God is the ultimate creator of all human life. The life which all men and women share is finally to be understood as a gift. Lastly, we continue to recognize a definite uniqueness in the way humanity and divinity came together in the person of Jesus. Humankind could never have achieved the new awareness of the intimate link between itself and God on its own. The explicit revelation of the Christ Event was an absolute necessity. While this Event now allows us to experience a new closeness with the creator God, our humanity will never share the intimacy with the divine nature in an identical way with Jesus.

This understanding of the ultimate significance of the Christ Event, not as the fulfillment of Jewish Messianic awareness but as proclamation of a new depth in the understanding of divine-human bonding, certainly must be seen as an outgrowth of developments within Second Temple Judaism, especially the whole thrust of the Pharisaic movement towards the sense of God as Father of each individual person. But it also represents a *novum* that neither Pharisaism nor any other branch of Judaism was quite prepared to accept. Here the perceptive words written by the late Rabbi Abraham Heschel remain very valid. Heschel had no hesitation in affirming that the notion of the Incarnation marked the point at which Christianity and Judaism part company spiritually, despite the presence in Judaism of a certain measure of "Incarnationalism." Biblical scholar James A. Sanders has in fact highlighted the Incarnational seeds in Heschel's own works.[30] But Heschel is firm in maintaining that the notion of the "sympathetic union" with God achieved by the Prophets of Israel must be clearly distinguished on the one hand from the mystical union where the person attains a state of identity with the divine and, on the other, from the notion of the Incarnation where the divine fully enters the human realm.[31] The human personality is not annihilated by the divine essence. On this point Heschel stands in complete agreement with Incarnational Christology. But neither can the human personality in anyway be identified with the divine essence according to Heschel. Here is where Incarnational Christology and his notion of "sympathetic union" sever ties. All that is possible from the Jewish perspective as understood by Heschel is a deep feeling of solidarity between the human community and the divine purpose, a solidarity that paves the way for an intensified form of divine-human partnership in which attainment of divine aims becomes inextricably linked to human co-operation and effort. Certainly such partnership is also part of the vision inherent in Incarnational Christology. But ultimately Incarnational Christology proclaims something beyond this without in anyway minimizing the importance of this partnership.

A number of further points need to be made here about this Incarnational uniqueness of Christianity vis-a-vis Judaism. In the first place, we have to reaffirm a point that was already stressed. The ultimate implications of Jesus' ministry culminating in his Death/Resurrection came only gradually. They were not fully evident at the outset of Jesus' public life, nor even at the end. As E.P. Sanders and other scholars have rightly argued, these developments took considerable reflection and soul-searching on the part of the apostolic community and, if we are to believe Raymond Brown, certain liturgical experiences as well. This fact has led certain Jewish scholars over the years to argue that Paul and the early Christian community basically perverted the es-

---

[30]"An Apostle to the Gentiles," *Conservative Judaism,* 25:1 (Fall 1973), 61-63.

[31]Cf. Fritz Rothschild (ed.), *Between God and Man.* New York: Free Press, 1959, 25. Also cf. Abraham Heschel, *The Prophets.* New York: Harper & Row, 1962.

sentially Jewish message of Jesus through the development of Incarnational Christology. Hyam Maccoby's *The Mythmaker: Paul and the Invention of Christianity*[32] is the most recent example of this rather classical Jewish thesis. While we Christians must acknowledge the development and not pretend that all Christological understanding was completely unfolded in Jesus' own teachings, we likewise recognize that the early church's varied attempts at formal theological statements about the Christ Event grew directly out of actions and words of Jesus himself as recorded in the gospels. The whole basis of Jesus' ministry in behalf of the outcasts of his day, his affirmation of human reconciliation as fundamental to authentic faith expression, his transfer of "divine" power to his disciples in the form of the authority to forgive sins and his willingness to see the Torah as sacred but not ultimate, all directly depended on a sense of a new dignity for humanity made possible through the personal link he sensed he shared in a unique way with the Father. The tragedy of later Christianity was that in continuing to refine this Incarnational vision, whose authentic roots lie in Jesus' ministry, it frequently lost completely Jesus' profound sense of the continuing sacredness of Torah Judaism. This is what the church has been attempting to reappropriate since Vatican Council II.

The second major point has to do with the relationship of Jesus' Death/Resurrection to Incarnational Christology and to a new theology of the Christian-Jewish relationship. Nearly all discussions of this issue have taken place within the context of the searing experience of the Shoah, the attempt by the Nazis to annihilate six million People. Out of reflections on this Shoah experience some Christian theologians have developed the premise that the most significant linkage between Christianity and Judaism is to be found through an association of Jesus' Crucifixion with the sufferings endured by the Jewish People during the Holocaust. Douglas Hall, for example, has argued that only a theology of the Cross preserves meaning for the Incarnation after the Shoah. This is the sole Christological interpretation to surface

---

[32]New York: Harper & Row, 1986.

the authentic divine-human link implied in the Word becoming flesh through its stress on the solidarity of God with suffering humanity.[33] Franklin Sherman takes a somewhat different, but nonetheless parallel approach. For him, the revelation of the cross is first and foremost the revelation of the fundamental *Jewish* reality of suffering and martyrdom of which the Shoah was the apex. Such a Cross-centered Christology will lead not to the traditional exclusion of the Jews from the salvation ambit but to a new sense of the profound bonding between the two faith communities under a God who has revealed to both his willingness to participate in the sufferings of his people.[34] The Israeli Catholic philosopher Marcel Dubois speaks in similar tones: "...the Calvary of the Jewish people, whose summit is the Holocaust, can help us to understand a little better the mystery of the cross.[35] Another Catholic sounding this note is Clemens Thoma: "Auschwitz is the most monumental sign of our time for the intimate bond and unity between the Jewish martyrs—who stand for all Jews—and the crucified Christ, even though the Jews in question could not be aware of it."[36]

The most thorough treatment of the link between a Cross-centered Christology and the Shoah to date is found in Jurgen Moltmann's volume *The Crucified God.* [37] For Moltmann the Shoah has uncovered the profoundest reality of the Christ Event—God can save people, including Israel, because through the Cross divine reality became permanently tied to human suffering in the most intimate of ways. For the church to continue theologizing after the Shoah would indeed prove a futile enterprise in Moltmann's perspective:

> ...were not the *Sch'ma Israel* and the Lord's Prayer in

[33]"Rethinking Christ," in Alan T. Davies (ed.), *Antisemitism,* 167-187.

[34]"Speaking of God After Auschwitz, " *Worldview,* 17:9 (September 1974). Also cf. Sherman's essay on the same theme in Paul D. Opsahl and Marc H. Tanenbaum (eds.), *Speaking of God Today.* Philadelphia: Fortress, 1974.

[35]Cf."Christian Reflection on the Holocuast."

[36]Clemens Thoma, *A Christian Theology,* 159; also cf. 3.

[37]New York: Harper & Row, 1978.

Auschwitz itself, were not God himself in Auschwitz itself, suffering with the martyred and murdered. Every other answer would be blasphemy. An absolute God would make us indifferent. The God of action and success would let us forget the dead, which we still can not forget. God as nothingness would make the entire world into a concentration camp.[38]

Moltmann adds that such a "theology of divine vulnerability" emerging from the Shoah has deep echoes in rabbinic theology and in Abraham Heschel's notion of *divine pathos* developed in his volume on the prophets.[39]

It can be said that Moltmann's theology of the Cross born out of his reflection on the Holocaust has introduced an important dimension of Incarnational Christology which may perhaps be shown ultimately to enhance Christianity's linkage with Judaism as he, along with Sherman, Thoma and Dubois, suggest. But we must tread with caution here. Moltmann's emphasis on the Cross, interpreted through the prism of the Shoah, as the central reality of Christology certainly brings to the fore the notion that God had to pay a price, as it were, for the freedom accorded humankind when this freedom suffered massive abuse during the Holocaust. In modifying exaggerated notions of divine omnipotence whose religious glorification often led segments of the human community to attempt false imitations of this supposed divine attribute by the use of power and domination in the social sphere, the theology of divine vulnerability helps to undercut the basis for classical theological and political antisemitism which, as Rosemary Ruether, Elisabeth Schüssler Fiorenza and David Tracy correctly argue, ultimately has an important part of its roots in this patriarchal mentality.[40]

If we come to an appreciation of the Christ Event as the

---

[38]"The Crucified God," *Theology Today,* 31:1 (April 1974), 9.

[39]Cf. *The Prophets.*

[40]Cf. Rosemary Ruether, *Faith and Fratricide* and Elisabeth Schüssler-Fiorenza and David Tracy, "The Holocaust as Interruption and the Christian Return to History," in Elisabeth Schussler-Fiorenza and David Tracy (eds.), *The Holocaust,* 83-86.

revelation that men and women can finally be healed in the deepest recesses of their consciousness, that they can once and for all overcome the primal sin of pride which manifests itself in the patriarchal desire to supplant the Creator in power and status because of the self-imposed divine self-limitation manifested through the Cross, then the church may have rid itself of the very basis of its displacement theology of Judaism which oppressed Jews for centuries and finally combined with pagan forces to produce the annihilation of six million Jews and millions of Poles, Gypsies, gays, and others. This is where Moltmann's theology becomes absolutely crucial, if ultimately incomplete as a full Christological model. It has now become possible for people to understand through the revelation of the Christ Event, which brought to a head an awareness already developing in Pharisaic Judaism, that their destiny is eternal in their uniqueness and individuality. God will not finally try to absorb them totally back into the divine being. In fact, it has become apparent that God must grant men and women this measure of perpetual distinctiveness and freedom in order to attain full maturity as Creator, to become finally and fully God. This is a Christological viewpoint that seems to bear some resemblance to the notion of divine self-constriction as integral to God's decision to create found in portions of the Jewish mystical tradition which grew up well after the birth of Christianity. It would prove useful to explore this possible connection at greater length as a potential source of theological cross-fertilization between Judaism and Christianity.

But honesty compels us to say that there are aspects of a Shoah-based Cross Christology that make the sensitive Christian quite uneasy. Can the Christian in good conscience combine the Cross Christology with the Holocaust knowing the significant complicity of baptized Christians in the Nazi program? A Roy Eckardt is especially adamant in rejecting such linkage as close to blasphemy. He also believes that "in comparison with certain other sufferings, Jesus' death becomes relatively non-significant." Another danger perceived by Eckardt in such a Christology is that it may generate an exaggeratedly "powerless" approach to morality which would prove suicidal for a threatened minority such as the Jews, but in the long run for the Christian community as well.[41] Additionally, Christian theology has traditionally spoken of Jesus' death on the Cross as a voluntary act on the part of both God and Jesus. The cross has also been interpreted in a redemptive vein when seen as the culmination and the consequence of Jesus' public ministry. The Shoah, on the other hand, was neither voluntary nor redemptive in any sense. So we can see why some Jews react quite negatively to the attempted association of Cross Christology with the Holocaust. Finally, some doubts have surfaced among scholars whether the purported ties between the theology of divine suffering present in parts of the Jewish tradition is really as close to the Holocaust-inspired Cross Christology as Moltmann and Sherman have argued.

Weighing the pros and cons, it still seems justified, and important, to stress Cross Christology in the effort at creating a new theological model for the Jewish-Christian relationship. Moltmann has captured a vital dimension of the authentic and unique revelation of the Christian covenant in *The Crucified God*. Whether it is proper to link this Christological reality to the Shoah still remains an open question in my judgment, though I am inclined against it. But, and this is an absolutely crucial modification, this Cross Christology cannot be presented as the ultimate and final revelation, but only as a central dimension of a broader reality that includes the perduring features of the permanent Jewish covenant as core elements as well.

A. Roy Eckardt's comment, written early in his dialogue career, remains very much to the point:

> If there is a true sense in which God has manifested himself uniquely in Jesus of Nazareth, it must be said that the mystery of this divine act is in principle no greater than the sacred acts through which Israel was originally elected.[42]

We will deal with this question in greater depth in the next

---

[41]"Christians and Jews Along a Theological Frontier," *Encounter*, 40:2 (Spring 1979), 102.

[42]*Elder and Younger Brothers*, 142.

chapter. At this point it is sufficient to emphasize that in any proclamation of Cross Christology as a pivotal aspect of the revelation in the Christ Event care must be exercised to show its connections with the growing awareness of divine-human intimacy in the Pharisaic Judaism that provided the context for Jesus' message as well as divine sufferings theme in the Hebrew Scriptures and the Jewish mystical literature. Also, the notion of salvation *within community,* so fundamental to the Jewish covenant and frequently neglected or underplayed in Christianity, must be presented in any such proclamation as an indispensable correlative of any Cross Christology.

We need now to turn our attention very briefly to the question of the Resurrection. Certainly this has been seen by much of Christian theology and piety as a distinguishing, if not the principal, characteristic of Christian faith vis-a-vis Judaism. As a result, a few of the most radical Christian theologians connected with the dialogue with Jews have called for the abandonment of classical Christian belief in the Resurrection. Rosemary Ruether argued in this vein in *Faith and Fratricide* with the premise that belief in the Resurrection led the church into a false sense of triumphalism that in turn parented its deep-seated anti-Judaism. "What Christianity has in Jesus," she asserts, "is not the Messiah, but a Jew who hoped for the kingdom of God and who died in that hope."[43]

Eckardt employs even stronger language than Ruether in insisting that rejection of the Resurrection doctrine is critical for any constructive development of a new theological model for the Jewish-Christian relationship. While not part of his initial writings on the topic, it has become very prominent in his more recent works, including his latest volume *Jews and Christians: The Contemporary Meeting.*[44] In Eckardt's eyes the Shoah finally doomed the resurrection doctrine for the church. This is not to say that it eradicated something that was *once* authentic, but rather that it exposed the fundamental error of that belief in the

---

[43]"An Invitation to Jewish-Christian Dialogue," 17.

[44]Bloomington, IN: Indiana University Press, 1986.

first place. At best, Eckardt maintains, Resurrection can have only a future connotation. All attempts at reinterpreting the Resurrection as theological symbol are bound to fail in Eckardt's judgment and he remains unconvinced as well by the effort of the dialogue scholar J. (Coos) Schoneveld to understand the event as a vindication of Jesus "as a Jew," and a confirmation of God's promises to the People Israel.[45]

In Eckardt's words:

> That Jewish man from the Galilee sleeps now. He sleeps with the other Jewish dead, with all the disconsolate and the scattered ones of the murder camps, and with the unnumbered dead of the human and non-human family. But Jesus of Nazareth shall be raised. So too shall the small Hungarian children who were burned alive at Auschwitz.[46]

This future resurrection of Jesus will carry special meaning for Christians because it is his history which enabled the Gentiles to enter the ongoing covenant with the Jewish People. In a parallel way the future resurrection of Abraham and Moses will have special significance for the Jewish eschatological community.

Nearly all other Christian scholars involved in the dialogue with the Jewish People have rejected this radical posture towards the Resurrection doctrine taken by Eckardt. But most are at least willing to grant he has raised a central question that needs further addressing. And, to some measure at least, most are prepared to acknowledge a pervasive triumphalism associated with the Resurrection doctrine which has seriously harmed the church, including the understanding of its ongoing link with the Jewish People. Though Eckardt has specifically rejected the following perspective on the Resurrection as just another form of Christian supercessionism (wrongly I believe),[47] there exists a definite possibility

---

[45]"The Jewish 'No' to Jesus," *Quarterly Review*, 52-63. For Eckardt's reactions, cf. *Jews and Christians*, 85-86.

[46]"The Resurrection and the Holocaust," Paper Presented to the Israel Study Group, New York, March 4, 1978.

[47]Cf. *Jews and Christians*, 145.

of preserving a Resurrection doctrine free of triumphalism in a reconstituted theology of the Jewish-Christian relationship. Key to such inclusion is an appreciation of the Pharisaic origins of the doctrine. Resurrection was one of the principal issues on which the Pharisees broke with other Jewish groups of the period, especially their archrivals the Sadducees. This is clear from the pages of the New Testament. For Pharisaism the notion of the resurrection was an outgrowth of their intensified sense of the depth of divine-human intimacy resulting from their view of God as Father.

Viewed in this context, then, the Christian notion of Resurrection regarding Jesus is not a proclamation of a "miracle" but a part of the larger Christian proclamation of Incarnational Christology. Jesus had to rise because of the fundamental reality he had proclaimed in his ministry and which the church had come to see in and through his person—humanity was an eternal dimension of divinity. So, contrary to Eckardt, Resurrection can be included in a new theological approach to Judaism that does not totally vitiate the latter's continuing role. This is possible so long as we do not make Incarnation/ Resurrection the totality of covenantal revelation, but only as an integral part (from the Christian perspective) of a larger revelational whole that includes the core elements of the Jewish covenant as equally important elements.

Understood as a derivative doctrine of the Incarnation, Resurrection becomes a powerful theological statement about the meaning of Jesus as well as the ultimate significance of humanity. Also, since the Incarnational process remains fundamentally incomplete, Resurrection becomes more of a future promise than a completely present reality. For the notion of resurrection within Pharisaism was intimately bound to Judaism's communal ethos. No individual person would enjoy the experience of resurrection from the Pharisaic perspective until the full community had reached the period of the Messianic end-time. Thus there was no basis for any form of triumphalism enroute. Sin, at its heart the struggle between Creator and creatures for supremacy, would in the end be resolved. Such was the promise inherent in Jesus' Resurrection. But it remained still by and large a promise, not completed reality. And this resolution would occur only through the active earthly cooperation of people to resolve the struggles and divisions still plaguing humanity.

Eckardt raises a further point relative to my approach to Resurrection which bears some comment because it leads right into another important issue in our overall discussion of a new theological model for the Christian-Jewish relationship. My continuing stress on Resurrection, even though it shuns the old triumphalism, in effect introduces a new strain of the disease, he argues, by "condemning the Jewish disallowance that a human being could be divine."[48] It is necessary to admit that the Incarnation/Resurrection doctrine does bring into the dialogue a motif which Judaism has traditionally rejected, though Pinchas Lapide has questioned this rejection in a controversial new volume.[49] But to say that Christianity has a unique revelation in and through the Christ Event is not automatically to engage in a triumphalistic putdown of Judaism if at the same time the church acknowledges the enduring, unique revelatory insights of the Jewish covenant. The conclusion that Eckardt draws from my effort relative to the Resurrection doctrine is not as inevitable as he claims.

But I must admit that Eckardt is quite correct in one respect, and the truth of his contention forces us to ask some basic questions about approaches to theological dialogue. In presenting my interpretation of the Incarnation/Resurrection doctrine there is indeed a sense in which I have "disallowed" what he and most Jews consider Judaism's traditional position about the absolute impossibility of divine-human interpenetration. In this sense I am professing my belief that *on this point* Christianity has moved beyond the pale of Judaism and done this correctly as a result of studied reflection on the basic meaning of Jesus' ministry culminating in the Easter events. Saying this does not fundamentally invalidate the Jewish covenant nor reduce Judaism to total inferiority vis-a-vis Christianity. It is only, but importantly, to say

---

[48]*Ibid.*

[49]*The Resurrection of Jesus: A Jewish Perspective,* trans. by Wilhelm C. Linss. Minneapolis: Augsburg, 1983.

that I remain convinced that Christianity has the more developed understanding in this regard, an understanding I deem vital for resolving important aspects of the human condition, and that is why I choose to remain a believing Christian rather than converting to Judaism. We must be clear about one point in the new Jewish-Christian encounter: the new theological model of its relationship to the Jewish People that the church is now slowly constructing will never be identical with the religious self-definition of a Jew. As close as they might come in many respects, the two theological definitions will inevitably separate on some crucial points.

It is precisely for this reason that I can lean towards the double covenant model. Most of the single covenant theologians examined in the first chapter simply have not done justice to the unique dimensions of Christianity which seem to be clearly present, however inchoatively, in the New Testament accounts of Jesus' ministry. In this regard the oft-repeated Jewish argument, recently reaffirmed in new books by Hyam Maccoby[50] and Stuart Rosenberg,[51] is highly exaggerated in its claim that Jesus was a perfectly good Jew whose basic teachings were perverted by the pagan Paul. It is true, and the truth is indeed painful and needs to be confronted by the church far more than it has up till now, that Christian uniqueness has often been stated in ways that lost all touch with its Jewish soul. This led to a false sense of Christian superiority that prove disastrous for Christian spirituality and for the very existence of the Jewish community. But acknowledging this does not imply that we must shun all statements of difference between Judaism and Christianity, which seems to be the logical conclusion of what Eckardt is saying even though he has never actually carried the thesis that far. The single covenant theologians such as van Buren simply have not done adequate justice to the uniqueness of the revelation in the Christ Event. Christianity is more than Judaism for the Gentiles, though,

---

[50] *The Mythmaker. Paul and the Invention of Christianity.* New York: Harper & Row, 1986.

[51] *The Christian Problem. A Jewish View.* New York: Hippocrene, 1986.

surely, in a most important way it is also that. And we must be grateful to the single covenant theologians for forcefully reminding us of this fact. Even the most comprehensive of the single covenant theologians, Paul van Buren, has failed to meet this test even though he has indicated on a number of occasions in his various writings that the church's appropriation of the original Jewish covenant through the Christ Event is somewhat different from its appropriation by Jews. The problem is that he has never spelled out this distinctive appropriation by Christians in any clear fashion.

But I cannot let most of the double covenant theologians off without some criticism of their position as well. The basic weakness of the leading figures of this school, such as Thoma and Mussner, is that they fail to develop a theology of Jewish uniqueness. What does Judaism have to offer Christianity in its continuing relationship with the church? This seems to me to be the second basic challenge of an adequate double covenant theology and here by and large the double covenant theologians have also fallen short. It is to this area that we shall briefly turn out attention in the final chapter.

Before turning to this very critical question of a Christian theology of Jewish uniqueness (if we may call it that), it is necessary to consider for a moment one additional point. It is the issue of supposed Christian "universalism," which so frequently has been used by the churches to denigrate Judaism because of its stress on particularity and thereby to highlight the apparent superiority of Christianity.

At the outset of the discussion it is necessary to repudiate clearly the usual Christian version of the universality/particularity contrast as a gross oversimplification of the reality of Judaism on the one hand and of actual Christian practice on the other. The universalistic/particularistic tension has been an ongoing debate in Judaism from biblical times to the present day.[52] And the fact is

[52]For the biblical period, cf. chapter 5 of my *Sinai and Calvary: The Meeting of Two Peoples.* Beverly Hills: Bruce & Glencoe, 1976. For examples of modern discussions cf. Irwin M. Blank, "The Covenantal People and the Righteous of All Nations," and William Cutter and Alan Henkin, "Universalism and Particularism: Where Ends and Means Collide, *Journal of Reform Judaism,* 26:2 (Spring 1979), 61-81.

that Judaism has integrated itself far more deeply into non-Western culture in periods when Christianity continued to show a distinctively alien Western face in these same lands. It is therefore quite incorrect for Christians to claim any endemic superiority in this regard. Professor Jacob Neusner, in fact, has argued that the early Christians, if one examines their theologies, consciously sought to imitate the ethnic character of Judaism. That is why, he claims, they began to speak of themselves as the "New Israel."[53]

On the theological level, I believe there remains some validity in contrasting Judaism and Christianity through the universal-particular model. The Pauline "In Christ there is neither Jew nor Greek" contains an important religious insight. Ultimately this insight is rooted in Jesus' decision to build community on the basis of the utter dignity of each individual person. In this light distinctions of race, nation and creed assume a secondary, though not unimportant, role. But, as James Parkes has noted, Jesus ultimately did no better than his Pharisaic counterparts in resolving the persistent individual/community tension in society. By grounding its religious faith in the solemn commitment to peoplehood, Judaism has been forced to struggle continually with the role of the "outsider" in its midst. The Christian church, on the other hand, has had to fight to maintain a communitarian ideal in the face of the ever-present threat of excessive individualism. The starting points are certainly different for each faith community. But, in the end, they are both challenged by the same basic questions.

This concludes our basic overview of Christology and Judaism. Many unanswered questions remain in contemporary Christianity's effort to define its own continuing uniqueness while at the same time allowing for the development of a constructive theology of Judaism. It is unlikely that these questions will be resolved in the near future. The process of theological reflection, a process that is in effect beginning where St. Paul left off in Romans 9-11, must continue for some time before issues will be clarified

[53]"Israel and the Nations," *CCAR Journal,* 17:3 (June 1970), 31.

sufficiently to gain a consensus viewpoint within the churches. But there is no doubt that further development of a Christian theology of Jewish uniqueness is an integral part of such ongoing reflection and such an ultimate consensus. It is to this problematic that we now turn in the following chapter.

3

Incarnational Christology and the Continuing Vitality of Judaism

The Christological direction emphasized in chapter two, the unique Incarnational dimension within a Pharisaic Jewish setting, inevitably leads to the question, what significance does the Jewish covenant retain in such a perspective? Some single covenantal Christian theologians such as Paul Van Buren would still regard such a perspective as laden with the seeds of traditional Christian supercessionism. This is admittedly not an easy question to address. For, as we indicated at the close of the previous chapter, this Christological vision does imply a degree of universalism. The nub of the issue would seem to come down to whether this admitted universal thrust in Incarnational Christology is all embracing and exclusivist. Is it a totally self-sufficient, self-sustaining notion or does it need to be complemented by other "universalist" elements, including ones crucial to the Jewish covenantal experience? Put another way, must we describe Incarnational Christology as a limited universalism? I think we must. That is why it can be reasonably argued that insistence on Christian uniqueness flowing from the Incarnational vision does not automatically rule out a constructive, ongoing theology of the Jewish People within the churches. The fundamental mistake of nearly all past Christologies has been to consider their unique Christological perspective as exclusively universal.

At this moment of religious history it is necessary for Christians to affirm that Judaism continues to play a unique and distinctive role of its own in the overall process of human salvation. Despite the biblical heritage that they share and Jesus' profound debt to Pharisaism, Judaism and Christianity developed into essentially distinct religions, each emphasizing different, though complementary, aspects of human religiosity. This viewpoint supports the contention of such Jewish scholars as the late Arthur Cohen and Hans Jonas that reference to a single Judaeo-Christian tradition represents a basic distortion of reality. In the course of history each has developed a distinctive ethos rooted in varied communal experiences. Authentic dialogue between them, and meaningful theological reflection on their relationship, must begin with the clear acknowledgement of this difference.

Central to Jewish covenantal faith has been the sense of peoplehood, of salvation in and through community. Judaism was profoundly convinced that no single individual could attain salvation until the entire human family had arrived at that sacred moment. Even the Pharisees, the most ardent champions of individualism within Judaism up till the Enlightenment, could not envision personal resurrection until the full reign of God had dawned for all. The fundamental religious reality for Judaism was the covenant between God and the People Israel. This became the barometer for evaluating Israel's future faith life, including some harsh judgments about it pronounced over the years by the prophets. That is why it is so significant that some recent theologians have returned to the centrality of the Sinai covenant in constructing their Christologies. This is an especially commendable dimension of certain liberation theologians such as Gustavo Gutierrez and Jose Miguez Bonino, despite some very serious shortcomings with regard to other aspects of their presentation of Judaism and its continuing relationship with Christianity.[1]

This fundamental revelation of salvation as ultimately communal must be seen by Christians as standing on equal footing with the revelation in Jesus. His coming in no way eradicated its ultimate significance. The revelation accorded the church in and through his teaching/person adds to, but does not obliterate, this first revelatory experience. Unfortunately Christianity frequently lost sight of this connection after its separation from the synagogue. The predominant influence of Hellenistic thought after the split often led the churches into an overly individualistic interpretation of the Incarnational revelation, in which people became convinced they could reach full communion with God by sidestepping or even deliberately isolating themselves from communal relationships.

A glaring illustration of this destructive individualistic tendency can be seen in the deterioration of Eucharistic celebration in Catholicism which has begun to be reversed only since the reforms of Vatican II. The Eucharist, communal at its very core, ought to be the ultimate symbol in the church of its conviction that people can only be saved in a communal context. It is a proclamation that people united become in a very real sense the body of Christ. Such a perspective stood at the heart of the mature Paul's Christology. It surely represented one of his most significant statements concerning the unity of humanity, its fundamental dignity and the ultimate bond between divinity and humanity. Yet this sacred and central biblical symbol, unlike the sabbath meal in which it had its roots, was allowed to degenerate into a privatistic I-God activity, a process we are beginning to reverse since the Council only with great difficulty. Here is a clear, concrete example of a difference in ethos between Judaism and Christianity.

Christianity may indeed continue to emphasize the centrality of the individual far more than Judaism. But

---

[1]Cf. *Christ in the Light,* 59-68.

ongoing Christian contact with Judaism is necessary for Christians to overcome this deep-seated and long-standing tendency towards false privatization of religion. Christianity stands in danger of losing its soul unless it retains a link to this particular revelatory dimension of Jewish covenantal faith.

A second way in which Jewish covenantal faith can help correct distortions in the Christian perspective is through the notion of Torah. Over the years Christianity has frequently been guilty of espousing inflated notions of human freedom supposedly based on Paul's rejection of the Jewish legal tradition. This has become a major focal point in contemporary liberation theology and historically it has preoccupied many European theologians, especially from the Protestant communities. It has also served as the basis for the destructive juxtaposing of Judaism and Christianity as religions of law and freedom respectively.

The overwhelming majority of Christian theologians have simply failed to grasp the richness inherent in the Jewish term "Torah" which is inadequately translated by the usual English term "law." Far too frequently the liberation Christians understand as integral to Jesus' message is described in very generic ways. In fact, authentic liberation will not come about in society until political/religious ideals have been transformed into concrete socio-cultural structures. This is precisely what the Torah process tried to accomplish. Jesus himself, given his close association with the Pharisaic movement, no doubt was deeply cognizant of this as his own invasion of the Temple precincts demonstrates. The notion of "oral Torah" that became pivotal for the reforms in Jewish society introduced by the Pharisees and advanced by Jesus and the early church certainly expanded the understanding of Torah inherited by Second Temple Judaism from the Hebrew Scriptures. But it did not totally replace the earlier Torah tradition.

Unlike Jesus and at least a part of apostolic Christianity, later church theology often lost touch with Torah tradition. This proved extremely harmful to its own spirituality, to say nothing of its relationship to the People Israel. The Christian-Jewish dialogue, by enabling Christians to appreciate more deeply the role of Torah, can aid the Church in moving away from mere generalized pronouncements about the freedom it has gained in and through the incarnational revelation towards actions that generate concrete liberating structures in human society. Far too often Christians naively express preference for the unspecified statements about freedom in Christ in the New Testament over the lists of "legal" requirements contained in the pages of the Hebrew Scriptures without realizing that a notion of freedom that does not bring us directly into the realm of concrete, human living, as the Torah process does, will prove terribly ineffective in the long run in terms of the actual realization of freedom. The Jewish understanding of Torah must certainly take its place as part of the unique dimension of Jewish covenantal faith within a Christian theology of Judaism.

Another critical dimension of the Jewish covenantal tradition that can have a positive impact on Christian faith is the sense of the human person as co-creator, as co-responsible for history and for the world God created. This notion of co-creatorship emerges both from the biblical tradition and from subsequent Jewish religious reflection, including the literature of the mystical tradition. It is a strongly emphasized feature of some leading contemporary Jewish theologians such as the orthodox thinker Joseph Soloveitchik.[2] Recently, it has become a central component of Catholic social ethics. Pope John Paul II gave it a major focus in his encyclical letter *Laborem Exercens* ("On Human Work") and it received important mention in the U.S. Bishops' Energy Statement (1981), their Peace Pastoral (1983) and in the Canadian Bishops' Statement on Economic Policy (1983). The Economics Pastoral released in 1986 by the U.S. hierarchy made co-creatorship a centerpiece of economic justice.[3]

---

[2]Cf. "Halakhic Man: Soloveitchik's Synthesis," in David Hartman. *A Living Covenant. The Innovative Spirit in Traditional Judaism.* New York: Free Press, 1985, 60-88.

[3]Cf. John T. Pawlikowski, "Participation in Economic Life," *The Bible Today,* 24:6 (November 1986), 363-370.

Critical for the reappropriation of this Jewish co-creatorship notion within the churches is the recognition that the salvation of humankind is primarily a task yet to be accomplished, that the Christ Event did not complete, but only advance, the process. The premature claims of Christianity for so long a time that the messianic kingdom had arrived fully in Jesus seriously eroded any feeling of responsibility for the destiny of the world. Now that the theological discussions among Christian scholars associated with the dialogue have resulted in the discarding of simplistic assertions about total fulfillment in Christ, as we saw in chapter one, Christians are confronted with the need to rediscover a faith basis for continued social involvement. Nothing will serve as a better bedrock for such a theology of justice than this biblically based theme of shared co-creational responsibilities between God and humankind.

The significance of this co-creational thematic cannot be overstated. More and more even official church pronouncements are seeing it as critical for contemporary social ethics. Though it has sometimes been criticized in extreme ecological circles as the root cause of Western exploitation of nature (a grossly exaggerated charge), it is in fact in the end a fundamental complement in a total vision of human dignity to the Incarnational revelation. As the discussion in the U.S. Economics Pastoral clearly shows, it is a biblical theme that is unique to the Hebrew Scriptures.

Another area in which the uniqueness of the Jewish covenantal experience can have a constructive impact on Christian faith is that of its basic outlook on the nature of the human person. Catholicism has been somewhat more positive on human nature than Protestantism over the course of centuries, but in the end both have tended to stress sinfulness rather than goodness in their theologizing on this point. Judaism has not been ignorant, of course, of a powerful sinful drive within human consciousness. But it views this drive as secondary in power to the "good inclination" in human beings, a drive that is activated primarily by conscious and deliberate choice rather than constituting a permanent mark of opprobrium.

Lack of contact with the Jewish and rabbinic viewpoints on human goodness by Christian theology for many centuries has resulted in a distorted emphasis on certain statements in the

Pauline writings without counterbalancing them with other parts of the Hebrew Scriptures and the New Testament. Some scholars such as Krister Stendahl,[4] now bishop of Stockholm, would even argue that later Protestant theologians projected back into Paul guilt feelings arising from their own introspection which were in fact foreign to Paul the Pharisaic Jew. As a result, there has been an exaggerated stress on the sinfulness of the human person in Christianity that can be modified through contact with the Jewish revelatory experience. While Judaism may need to do further, in-depth reflection on the innate power of evil in light of the Shoah experience, Christianity's approach stands in even greater need of correction. Since so much of Christianity's outlook on human sinfulness, especially in Catholicism, has been related to the area of sexuality, increased interchange with the Jewish tradition may help restore the far more positive outlook on human sexual activity as an avenue for experiencing the divine presence found in both the Hebrew Scriptures and the later Jewish mystical tradition.

A connected issue that can be raised here is that of the Christian understanding of forgiveness of sin and, for sacramentally based Christian denominations, the sacrament of Penance. For centuries the understanding and liturgical celebration of forgiveness has focused on the cleansing of the individual sinner from the stain of sin. This rather distorted interpretation of forgiveness and the sacrament of Penance was due in large part to the teachings of the Irish monks in the pre-medieval period. Unfortunately they took the church's understanding of forgiveness far afield, severing it from its roots in the Jewish tradition where it involves reconciliation with the person or persons affected by one's sinful action rather than inner cleansing. The New Testament in its account of the return of the Prodigal Son and its injunction not to dare to offer gifts at the alter until one has made amends with the person against whom the sinful deed has been directed carries on this authentic Jewish

[4]"The Apostle Paul and the Introspective Conscience of the West," *Harvard Theological Review* 56 (July 1963), 199-216.

spirit. We can hope that Christians will rediscover this original understanding of forgiveness and Penance through their new encounter with the uniqueness of the Jewish covenantal experience.

The final issue I will raise with regard to a preliminary theology of Jewish uniqueness is the land tradition of Judaism. Christian scholars such as Walter Brueggemann and W.D. Davies have completed important studies on this issue in recent years.[5] It is not possible here to go into the details of their analysis. Both assert, however, that failure to grasp the insights of this land tradition not only leaves Christians with a falsified picture of Judaism but also deprives Christianity of a vital rootedness in history and of a full appreciation of the role of the rest of creation in the emergence of God's final reign. While I would continue to maintain that there remain fundamental differences between Christianity and Judaism regarding the present meaning of the land tradition, differences ultimately rooted in Christianity's Incarnational revelation,[6] the church's faith must always be firmly entrenched in the earth. Far too often, concentration on the "heavenly Jerusalem" as a supposed replacement for the Jewish "earthly Jerusalem" has led to an excessively ethereal spirituality in the churches.

Brueggemann writes partially in reaction to the school of New Testament exegesis associated with the German scholar Rudolf Bultmann, whom he holds responsible for much of the loss of the land tradition in recent Christian theology. This Bultmannian hermeneutic focused on the personal, existential meaning of New Testament passages with an emphasis on instantaneous, radical decisions of obedience. Little room was left in such a perspective for the land tradition. The central problem for Christians, as Brueggemann explains it, "is not emancipation but *rootage,* not meaning but *belonging,* not separation from community but *location* with it, not isolation from others but *placement* deliber-

---

[5]Walter Brueggemann, *The Land.* Philadelphia: Fortress, 1977; W.D. Davies, *The Gospel and the Land.* Berkely: University of California Press, 1974 and *The Territorial Dimension of Judaism.* Berkeley: University of California Press, 1982.

[6]Cf. *Christ in the Light,* 127-33.

ately between the generation of promise and fulfillment."[7] Both
the Hebrew Scriptures and the New Testament, Brueggemann
maintains, present homelessness as the central human problem.
They seek to respond to it in terms of promise and gift. No truly
believing Christian can avoid making land a principal category in
his or her belief system. On this point Brueggemann is unbending.
"Landed" faith is as much an imperative for Christians as it is for
Jews.

W.D. Davies nuances the required Christian appropriation of
the biblical land tradition much more than Brueggemann. Davies
feels that when all is said and done the New Testament must be
described as ambivalent regarding the land promises found in the
Hebrew Scriptures. Strata exist within the New Testament that
take a critical view of these promises, and one passage (Acts 7)
rejects it outright. But other passages are to be found where the
land, the Temple, and Jerusalem in a clearly geographical sense
are looked upon quite positively in terms of their continued
meaning for the Christian gospel.

The New Testament, Davies concludes, leaves us with a
twofold witness with respect to the land tradition. On one hand,
there is a sense in which faith in Christ takes the believer beyond
the land, Jerusalem, and the Temple. Yet its history and theology
cannot escape concern about realities. In the New Testament,
holy space exists wherever Christ is or has been. The Christ Event
has "universalized" the land tradition in a significant way, but it
has not eliminated its centrality. Davies would no doubt concur
with Brueggemann that the Bultmannian approach is very mis-
guided in this respect. Davies summarizes the impact of the Christ
Event on the land tradition in this way:

> It (i.e., the New Testament) personalizes "holy space in Christ,
> who, as a figure of history, is rooted in the land; he cleansed the
> Temple and died in Jerusalem, and lends his glory to these and
> to the places where he was, but, as Living Lord, he is also free
> to move wherever he wills. To do justice to the personalism of

---

> the New Testament, that is, to its Christocentricity, is to find
> the clue to the various strata of tradition that we have traced
> and to the attitudes they reveal: to their freedom from space
> and their attachment to spaces. [8]

There is yet one other way in which contact with the land dimension of the unique Jewish covenantal tradition can enhance Christian faith expression today. In much of Christian liturgy we have lost almost all consciousness of the need to proclaim the glory of creation. Our Christian liturgical cycles tend to be virtually bereft of any festivals which highlight God's continuing presence in nonhuman creation. Such sensitivity must be re-claimed by Christians if the churches are to assume a leadership role in protecting our ecological heritage.

Before bringing to a close this brief examination of what elements might reasonably constitute a Christian theology of Jewish uniqueness, three concluding points are very much in order. First of all, it needs to be stressed that the approach taken in this chapter in no way implies that Judaism exists merely for the purpose of Christian faith completion. As Cardinal Joseph Bernardin of Chicago declared in a November 1984 address to the American Jewish Committee, Judaism carries ongoing theo-logical meaning in its own right apart from any significance it continues to have for Christian faith. Jews do not need Christian affirmation for their own faith integrity.

Secondly, Christians must be careful how they employ the term "people of God" in their theological statements. Though this term is important in restoring a communal context to Christian faith, after its break with Judaism the church has frequently lost sight of the fact that it must be used in a way that unambiguously affirms that Jews also remain "people of God." This central Vatican II image of the church must never be allowed to serve as the vehicle of Christian theological imperialism vis-a-vis the People Israel. Biblical scholar and ecumenist Gerald S. Sloyan forcefully underscores this point in an essay written several years ago:

---

[8] *The Gospel*, 367.

The very eagerness of the Christian bodies to employ the term "people of God" to describe themselves only is an indication of how little alerted they are to their own coming to birth from a Jewish mother who continues in good health. The problem is therefore as much one of an understanding in depth of Christian origins as it is of ecumenical relations with Jews.[9]

Finally, there will be need for some theological rethinking by Jews of their faith perspective on Christianity. While we must avoid at all costs trying to make dialogue look like a "quid pro quo" relationship, and while the problems are far greater and more urgent on the Christian side, nonetheless Jews cannot continue to applaud the developments in Christological rethinking we have discussed in the first two chapters without acknowledging that sooner or later these changes, if accepted by Christianity at large, will force Jews to reconsider some of their traditional outlooks on the Jewish-Christian bond from their side.

Some Jewish scholars have already begun this process.[10] They are to be commended for their efforts. Thus far these initial reflections have not matured to the point where any initial consensus has developed. But the caution introduced by Rabbi Gordon Tucker in an address several years ago to the International Conference of Christians & Jews Meeting near Florence, Italy, merits direct quotation. For, not only does it generally follow the track suggested in chapter two, but it also serves as a concluding reminder that we cannot expect the new theological discussions spoken of in this volume to produce dramatic breakthroughs in a short time. It will take a great deal of

[9]"Who are the People of God?", in Asher Finkel and Lawrence Frizzell (eds.), *Standing Before God.* New York: Ktav, 1981, 113.

[10]Cf. Walter Jacob, *Christianity Through Jewish Eyes: The Quest for Common Ground.* Cincinnati: Hebrew Union College Press, 1974 and Eugene B. Borowitz, "Jesus the Jew in Light of the Jewish-Christian Dialogue," *Proceedings of the Center for Jewish-Christian Learning,* College of St. Thomas, St. Paul, 2 (Spring 1987), 16-18. Also cf. my essay, "The Challenge of Jesus the Christ for the Synagogue," in *Proceedings,* 28-31. For a somewhat different approach but in the same general framework, cf. Joseph P. Schultz, *Judaism and the Gentile Faiths. Comparative Studies in Religion.* Rutherford, NJ: Associated University Presses, 1981.

patience and prolonged scholarly commitment to continue the process:

> The reinterpretation of Christian and Jewish ideas of covenant that have been developed by Paul van Buren, John Pawlíkowski, and Jacob Agus, among many others, have done an enormous amount to promote sensitive, less exclusionary perspectives on one another. But just as our differences should not be overemphasized, neither should our similarities, if only because they will not go away. The fact remains that Judaism and Christianity are very different religious types. Our histories and developments have proceeded along distinct tracks for 1800 years. We have different collective memories, different ways of structuring space and time, and different expectations for the end of days. Those are not trivial differences. They are almost "constitutional" in nature, "hard-wired" into us.